— R. Larry H

God Loves You!

Paul's Pastoral Passages Of Promise

Sermons On The Second Readings For Advent, Christmas, And Epiphany

11/4/10

Cycle B

Donald Charles Lacy

Donald Charles Lacy

CSS Publishing Company, Inc., Lima, Ohio

PAUL'S PASTORAL PASSAGES OF PROMISE

Copyright © 2007 by
CSS Publishing Company, Inc.
Lima, Ohio

Scripture quotations are from the New Revised Standard Version of the Bible, copyright 1989 by the Division of Christian Education of the National Council of the Churches of Christ in the USA. Used by permission.

For more information about CSS Publishing Company resources, visit our website at www.csspub.com or email us at csr@csspub.com or call (800) 241-4056.

Cover design by Chris Patton
ISBN 13: 978-0-7880-2517-4
ISBN 10: 0-7880-2517-1   PRINTED IN USA

Dedicated to
the United Methodist Church
of Yorktown, Indiana

Table Of Contents

Sermons For Sundays
In Advent, Christmas, And Epiphany
Paul's Pastoral Passages Of Promise
by Donald Charles Lacy

Preface

It is a joy to present this volume to clergy and laity alike. It is my tenth book of sermons, seven of them for CSS Publishing. I trust these pages will come alive for the reader's nourishment, especially providing ideas for speaking and writing.

The Advent/Christmas/Epiphany season is indeed a precious time for all adherents of the Christian faith. The texts, almost totally from Paul, offer special opportunities and challenges for us as we live out our lives in this always surprising world. At the beginning of the church year, the foundation is laid for future growth, offering unlimited potential for Christ and his church.

Generally, sermons are intended to put both pastor and people in touch with the living joys and concerns of the faith. For us who preach and write sermons over the years, it is so refreshing and exciting to experience the Word of the Living God speaking to us here and now.

While I have published well over 100 sermons, the next one being preached and written is always potentially the best one. In this case, Paul's pastoral passages of promise are placed before you in an "attitude of gratitude." Furthermore, I hope and pray they will help you cope with today's often hectic circumstances.

I especially want to recognize the United Methodist Church of Yorktown, Indiana, where I spent four beautiful years among loving, caring, and sharing people. I am indebted to their administrative secretary, Judy Marsh, for preparing this manuscript.

May the Holy Spirit abide with you, provide for you, and guide you now and forevermore.

Donald Charles Lacy

Advent 1
1 Corinthians 1:3-9

Thanksgiving And Thanksliving

Introduction
Don't you just love times of thanksgiving? Yes, and Saint Paul is a genius at reminding us of this component to victorious living. His "attitude of gratitude" finds its way throughout his letters, except possibly for Galatians.

My first response to all of this is "what a wonderful way to live our lives." Of course, he is rooted and grounded in his Savior and Lord. It is a natural — most likely spontaneous response — to the depths he discovers in Jesus.

Perhaps the most missing ingredient among those who profess the faith, is thanksgiving. In short, there appears to be a generous amount of complaining with loads of dissatisfaction, even among God's elect.

If God has truly come to us in flesh and blood as a Jewish male, we are the most blessed of all peoples. For the opportunity is at hand to receive the Messiah. Mary's son makes his entry and we have the great privilege of saying "Yes" to him.

Why should anyone who has received him be dejected and without hope? We know Paul's answer. There should be continued thanksgiving but that's not all. There must be thanksliving as well. Don't they belong together?

Focus
Thanksgiving and thanksliving are supposed to exist at the same time.

Body

1. Wholeness and holiness are manifested to the community at large.
Pause and reflect on your parish or parishes. Isn't the coming of Jesus Christ historically and personally a cause for precious people to become much less fragmented? With the potential of total integration we can observe at times our people becoming not only whole but holy. Thanksgiving reigns in the hearts and minds of parishioners, as this happens. Talk about being born again and again! Some will even exclaim, "I don't know him or her anymore!" A new human being emerges and a new personhood never witnessed before is there for all to see. Then we rediscover the magnificent power of our faith.

But that's not all. Pastors who know their flocks well see this happen — and indeed are a part of this — at a congregational level. Each church has a personality all its own. People become one in community. Old First Church that used to be that grouchy and stalemated organism becomes a unique creation. The old has gone and the new has come! It is much less interested in projecting a proper image and far more concerned about something (someone) else. The wholeness and holiness comes not so much in radical changing of structures as it does in experiencing the vitality of openly expressing thanksgiving born of thankful hearts and minds.

While I believe deeply in the spiritual changes occurring in an individual, there is always that further step to the entire community. A Christian in isolation is a contradiction in terms. Even those cloistered bear responsibility for making contributions to others. Their thanksgiving is also thanksliving as it rubs off on others in a monastery or convent. The greatness found in these institutions is always somehow and some way been in a body of people living in Christ. Such people as Thomas Merton are internationally known. However, that does not mean they were formed in a vacuum. They were invariably in contact and some relationship with their brothers or sisters. Wholeness and holiness has a way of rubbing off!

Can we apply this to denominations as well? I believe so. The Wesleyan family can point to John and Charles Wesley. It was obvious to them that the Church of England in their day and time had drifted far from a sense of serious Christianity. It needed to be made whole and holy again! So they sought to bring about needed changes. Their successes are legendary. While this eventually meant a new denomination, that was never the intent of the Wesley brothers. Some years ago, I met the Archbishop of Canterbury (George Carey) who indicated to me one of the worst things the Church of England ever did was to let those Methodists get away. Perhaps we should recognize we Methodists are in need of recapturing the emphasis on the Eucharist taught and practiced by the Wesleys. Then thanksgiving and thanksliving will come in a new thankful way.

2. Thanksgiving is intended to be extended.

"The testimony of Christ," as Paul says, means spiritual gifts are among us. The babe who was born in Bethlehem has provided us through the Holy Spirit a means of telling others. This within itself is one of the gifts. Our culture, just like others who have followed Christ, tends to surround us and even engulf us. This means our communicated testimony can be seriously influenced by matters such as bad timing, indifference, hesitancy, and incompetence. For those dear people who are spiritually oriented, such considerations can be seriously overrated. At the same time we are called to be cognizant of everything that will aid us in our mission to share. Thanksgiving and thanksliving.

Holding back or limiting the story and power of the faith can be tragic. We have this timeless gift in the person of Jesus the Christ to share with others. Our beginning point can be his birth to a Jewish maiden and all that surrounds this one of a kind breaking into history. After all, who wants to shun a lovely and holy young woman's baby boy? There is a certain magnetism about this special event that has been on the world scene for most of 2,000 years. Our destiny is tied to this little fellow, who comes among us as a human being. We have received in thanksgiving and we are called to share him in thanksliving. The angels sing and we shout, "Joy to the world!"

"To keep something you have to give it away" is a cliché that bears repeating. I believe this is especially true of the faith we proclaim. It sounds like Paul was much in agreement. Even as we acknowledge this, it can be one of the hardest things — in fact — to do. If something is really valuable to us, sometimes it is only in real hesitancy we share it with anyone else. That's the way we are and yet the Christian dynamic enables to see the imperative of such a matter. We have this treasure we are called to spread around, as the Holy Spirit directs. In particular, we do this by interacting with others. Paul says, "In every way you have been enriched by him, in speech and knowledge of every kind." Yes, it is time for "show and tell!"

"Extension ministries" or something similar is common terminology to most of us. Usually this means a position beyond serving the local church. While it seems accurate enough in terms of institutions and categories, I like to consider all ministry as an extension into the lives of people. That may sound "picky" until we see our understanding can be one of a local congregation being mostly static, raising money for those ministries considered "extension." The implication of that is a subtle way of blighting a much more thorough and complete "outreach!" Ponder that for a moment. You may discover our church has taken the easy way out!

3. A truly grateful person spontaneously desires to share.

Ideally, in the hearts and minds of Christians is an unending flow of "great thanksgivings." This is seen so distinctly in the writings of the Apostle Paul. It seems as though he can't stop giving thanks, especially for what he has found in Jesus the Christ. He overflows with expressions that inspire us, as well as other readers for centuries. He does so, even though clouds of imprisonment and shipwreck hang over him. He is the "Apostle of Gratitude" *par excellence.* The source is found in the Lord Jesus Christ. There is nothing fabricated or questionable about all of this. It is just there and he wants others to know.

If you are like I am, sometimes I get impatient with those who provide an artificial and syrupy thankfulness. It seems they are trying too hard to evidence something that just isn't there. The mere reading of this text does not mean we automatically capture the spirit of it. There is a spirituality at work calling for our entire being to shout into the heavens and also among our fellow women and men. It is getting beyond theory that counts in the long run. Genuine thanksgivings born of a right relationship with God the Father through his Son cannot be faked! Paul understood so well it is in paying the price for us by Jesus of Nazareth that the door opens to an "attitude of gratitude." Rejection and/or indifference speak for themselves.

Isn't it amazing what we communicate, often without knowing it? "He will strengthen you to the end, so that you may be blameless" is not for the light-hearted and those espousing a minimal Christianity. It is my experience we do not often fool "the world," so to speak, in our thankful expressions. If we really ascribe to Paul's approach, which means to live for Christ is also to die for him, even hardened secularists silently applaud our style. It is our spontaneity that sells others. There is nothing quite like a disciple who tells others how grateful he or she is for Christ and his church. "Sinners" may know a great deal more about the quality of our faith than we are willing to admit.

A thankful style of living that exudes from our innermost being is an evangelistic program all by itself. In a striking and masterful way, others catch this spirit in time and some even say excitingly they want what we have. It can even be reminiscent of the very early followers, who evoked a response from pagans saying, "See how those Christians love one another." No writer or painter can adequately depict such gloriously delightful scenes. That's how Christianity is supposed to work. Others are to seize our spirit, especially because our witness is unfeigned and inspirationally natural. The best sermons are those when few — if any — words are spoken and the power of the living God descends upon the moment. Great laity at times have to show clergy how and why this happens.

4. The world yearns for those who practice what they preach.

"Hypocrisy" is such a nasty word! In my long pastoral ministry of well over forty years I have come into contact with numerous people who spend virtually a lifetime dealing with it. They always seemed to look upon the lives of church people they knew and said — in one way or another — the Christian faith isn't lived.

They go to church and go through the motions; then on Monday a different life is lived. While we may say that is no justification for shying away from Christ, the point is well taken. There are those who seriously search for the power and purity of the gospel message. Sadly, often they do not seem to find it in their church-going neighbors and friends.

The hunger for genuine and vital Christian living is all about us. People feel — sometimes deeply — a void in their lives. Some read everything they can find on spirituality and do all the one/two principles. The discovery is made but the void is still there. Their search for "the grace of God that has been given you in Christ Jesus" eludes them. Books, various other publications, videos, and television/radio become more entertainment that anything else. What does the latest guru — Christian or non-Christian — say? Show them one solid honest-to-goodness disciple of Christ and lives can be changed overnight. The veneers and fabrications slip into the background. Thanksgiving and thanksliving become flesh and blood.

Perhaps the worst offenders of putting faith and practice together are clergy. Laying aside the political realities of the parish life, our people want to experience pastors who are thankful and live in that mood. Such sends an aroma throughout the parish. Even those who dislike us will honor and respect our styles of living. Our failures along this line are frequently closely related to upward mobility as professionals. We try too hard to succeed in wrong ways and end up failing in matters that really are crucial. I do not believe there is a more serious vocation or profession than being a clergyperson. We "walk the walk and talk the talk" or we become "a noisy gong or a clanging symbol."

In recent years, we have learned the mission fields are not abroad. They are next door, down the block, in the office, and at the coffee shop. Some who reside near us have even lost or never had the vocabulary to talk about Christ and his church. American culture has so changed in a couple of generations, that we can be caught off guard. Saint Paul was close to his churches and he taught them carefully and thoroughly about his Lord. They, too, faced a predominantly secularized society and emerged time and again faithful to what Paul taught them. We have come so far now that competing theologies even tend to blur any solid teaching we have for the world. We need to learn from the foreign mission fields the fact that we are all in this together. Go next door and proclaim Christ not Methodism!

Summary And Conclusion

So, "what has been joined together, let not man put asunder" is excellent advice. Thanksgiving and thanksliving belong together in one workable way of living. There is both substance and style. The legitimacy for this is a heavenly mark on our foreheads. We drink deeply and eat with inspired selection. Jesus and his ways are born among us and we are reminded of both his birth physically and our birth spiritually. Praise God we don't have to live with a set of principles. We can date our rebirth to his flesh and blood coming among us through blessed Mary. It is a relationship that never grows old. It is a highly productive marriage that passes from generation to generation.

Near the center of the city in Dallas, Texas, is an area called "Thanksgiving Square." It is a witness to the sameness of the world's religions at one point. All of them — in some form — espouse thanksgiving. It is a very moving experience to be there and share what seems to be something akin to holy ground. As you and I go about our lives, calling upon the wisdom of Saint Paul, just maybe life becomes worth living in ways we had only wondered about. Every community can have a thanksgiving square that is committed to Christian discipleship and interreligious dialogue with those who do not see things the way we do. We are so privileged to know the route of the babe in Bethlehem open to us.

Taking The Long View

___

Introduction

So much seems to press upon us in our daily living that "taking the long view" may not only be remote but considered impractical and therefore shelved. A thousand years equals one day and one day equals 1,000 years. It all sounds so mystical and unscientific! Do you mean we have to rethink being captains of our own ships? That is so basic to the American way and you are suggesting we give it up? After all, we can accomplish anything we set out to do — that is if we just try hard enough. Planning is done and realizable results in a given time frame are necessary.

Well, as some of us have learned, God does not see things and people the way we do. Whether it is Jesus' first or second coming, it happens on God's terms. I have heard it said some have been greatly disappointed he chose the particular time he did to bring his Son into the world. Why couldn't that have happened in time and space that was not nearly as male-oriented, even dominated? Equality of the sexes, especially in religion, could have thrived at a different time and place. Why didn't he return to us during the Second World War or some other cataclysmic moment in history? But he didn't.

Focus

We must seek to view things the way God does.

Body

1. Our God is before the beginning and after the ending.

As this soaks into our limited brains, we begin to have — at least — a clue to his bigness and our littleness. After all, aren't we supposed to do our measuring in starting and stopping points? To view life, especially cherished projects, in any other way is to ask for trouble. The boss sets goals and limits. We had better abide by them or, sooner or later, get fired. It really isn't going to help much to plead our case by maintaining, "But, God doesn't see it that way!" To live in a real world demands we adjust to the ways and means of the workaday world. Some people have to be kept happy, just for us to support our families. God may be God, but tell that to General Motors!

Questing of the sort the writer is speaking can be placed in a corner of the mind and never called upon again. It is labeled miscellaneous and perhaps even hurtful to one's progress. Before "the beginning and after the ending" is for a handful of philosophers to meditate upon. For John Q. Public and those primarily interested in "running the show" it is nothing more than unwanted stretching that goes no place. In truth the man or woman of faith is always more or less influenced by the idea presented. What appears to be so impractical must be considered for the health of our souls.

Could it be our real value and destiny are tied to the God who takes a view we cannot begin to measure? The words, "is patient with you, not wanting any to perish, but all to come to repentance" enter the picture. If he operated on our timetables, even our own salvation would be in jeopardy. In revival meetings I used to hear as a boy fiery evangelists say — in effect — be born again here and now or run the risk of spending eternity in hell. Frankly, such words scared me half to death! Emotions ran high and the old-fashioned mourner's bench was in clear view. God had spoken and no other chance to come to terms with him would be given.

Even after retirement, patience is often in short supply. The grandeur of the Creator with all his omnipotence and omniscience begs to be heard and believed. There are competitors. If I live ten more years, how much money will I need? Will my children pay

20

attention to me as I am restricted to a nursing home? All this grandeur stuff is fine but who is going to pay the bills? It seldom seems to occur to us that God is God and sooner or later he supplies our needs. We don't want to be dependent on anyone and that is understandable. Yet, if God has taken care of you for seventy, eighty, or even ninety years, won't he continue to do so? Are faith, hope, and love mere words that begin to dissolve as we get so old? The text says, "regard the patience of our Lord as salvation."

2. Our God created time and therefore is master of it.

This thought can be life-changing! To begin to probe an infinite mind that knows no beginning and ending and — in fact — creates what we understand as time itself has a jarring effect. In a way it is much like a spectacular trauma carrying the revelation of God's greatness clearly exceeding our boundaries. Adjustments to this can be a conversion experience. Our measuring sticks tend to become laughable, as we get a peak at the long view. Clocks and all time pieces seem so trivial; yet we know we must cling to them in order for our brief life on this earth to go on.

To look into the heavens with the psalmist and worship God the Father who gave us Jesus the Christ in the form of a baby strains our ability to articulate. That foremost of all babies became a part of time that God created. It is as though he utilizes his powers in such a way that Jesus becomes compliant to the Father's wishes. In still another way, the ages come together to provide humankind's Savior. It is enough to give us a headache, isn't it? It is as though God refuses to allow what he has created to get in the way of his Son's entrance. So, Mary is utilized with her permission to conceive and bear a child in time and yet out of time for he is the second part of the Eternal Trinity.

Regardless of the period in which we are born, live, and die, the long view soon catches up with us. We eventually recognize we are "dust and shall return to dust." We also are alerted to an undying soul, created by the *Almighty*, that has life beyond our measurements. God set the perimeters. Then we discover he is Master, regardless of time or lack of it. For the Christian this is very comforting because we can rest in the assurance love is at

21

work, especially in the birth, death, and resurrection of the Christ. Our hope is in the everlasting love of God the Father, Son, and Holy Spirit. Our souls are worth more to God than we can comprehend.

The persistence and consistency of such a view envelops both the good and evil. Struggle as we may, this Creator is at every turn. Our calling is to be found "without spot or blemish." Our free will, also given by him, is exercised and hopefully in ways that promise an eternal home. If it seems we are being crushed by all of this, in a way we are. Nevertheless, our assurance is found in him who goes to prepare a place for us. If a place is prepared for us, then he will come again and take us unto himself. Mystery in all of this comes and goes. We are able to see in a mirror dimly. What more can we ask? Our destiny is at stake and who better to trust than the God who created time and is master of it? As we struggle less and appreciate more, our death becomes powerfully positive.

3. Our God yearns for his children to catch a glimpse of his all-knowing powers.

The Almighty allows you and me the freedom to explore his greatness. We seem often afraid of all of this and end up either in predestination or license! Nevertheless, the windows of opportunity come and go, as we live out our lives. Each and every moment of the day (night) provides something or someone to aid us in a partial understanding of not only the creative process but of salvation history as well. Of course, we have to be alert and sensitive. This may or may not mean the disruption of our vocations and professions. The point is the ongoing availability of potential discovery in all our lives.

Just where is Jesus the Christ in all of this? Well, if God comes to us in flesh and blood in the person of Mary's baby, then he has a great deal to say. Our Lord's birth, ministry, crucifixion, resurrection, and ascension all enable us to catch a special glimpse. The privileges herein are remarkable for those who profess his name and seek to live by his commandments. In fact, they are unlimited! When we are ready to give up in attempting to make sense of life (and death), where do we go? We go to Rabbi Jesus. Through the Holy Spirit the needed understanding of the Father's will and ways are forthcoming. That does not necessarily mean clarity and specificity. It does mean an abiding presence that motivates us forward and upward.

Debates have raged for centuries about God's action or lack of action. As we live longer and are more absorbed in the Christian faith, I believe there is a certain peace that settles in. We hope we can live one more day but are thoroughly convinced we are not going to live 1,000 years in this life. In our twenties with — major and miraculous — medical advances we thought ten centuries was a possibility! I do not view this as resignation. If it is, it is a special type of succumbing to who and what God was, is, and shall be. Cynicism may rear its weighty head, but for those rooted and grounded in the faith, this is passing. The Father of our Savior and Lord will do whatever he chooses to do — whether it suits our fancy or not.

It seems to me the nature of God is such that we sooner or later pick up the truth that he seeks to woo us to him. Some would say this is a weakness and wishful thinking. It is put in the category of him laughing and crying. Perhaps such people would much rather deal with a first cause that simply does not communicate with his creatures. This denies the humanity of the one who created all of us and comes to us in the person of a baby, born of a woman. "Behold, I stand at the door and knock" is not an empty phrase that depicts a human god, devoid of any real power. It is a cardinal illustration of someone whose vast powers tell us there is providential care and concern, coming to us in a form we can understand.

4. Our God knows us thoroughly and totally, but respects our free will.

We are to "strive to be found by him at peace, without spot or blemish." Striving means it is definitely — to some extent — our doing. Our spiritual formation in the likeness of Christ may very well be a gift but our cooperation is imperative. God does not force his will upon us. In the end, of course, his will is done but let that not be a means to shove responsibility and even authority aside in our pilgrimage. As we, clergy and laity, labor to become more like our master, there is a certain grace that appears. It is as though our destiny is determined by the cooperation of God and man. Give thanks!

A real shocker is forthcoming as it dawns upon us the truth of the Creator's omniscience. Our privacy becomes non-existent. All that we do, say, and think is seen by the one who gave us life. For some this comes early in life and for others quite late. Then, I suspect for some it never comes at all. That is of tragic proportions! What do you mean there is some god out there who knows everything about me? That is sheer nonsense! Well, we know in the deepest part of our beings this is not all nonsense. The everlasting one who put us together in our mother's womb knows everything about us from conception. Is that something that should cause us to be in constant fear? Perhaps the best answer is: only if we belligerently insist on our unenlightened ways.

I am among those who find great comfort in God's knowledge of me. In that approach I discover his love and power coming together for my own good. Do I want it any other way? Frankly, the answer is, "No." There is grand joy. Only the one God of us all has the stature for this. Turn your imaginations loose and ponder a different arrangement. Are you willing to be tossed to and fro by elements and spirits? Are you really the captain of your own ship? In our prayers it helps to put in the beginning words which are obvious. Lord, you know all about me. Once this is unequivocally admitted, prayers take on the clothes of universal and personal reality. We know where we stand!

In the "long view" how much should others know about us? Having dealt with God's complete information bank on us, there is this related question. The sheer fact of the matter is that we are seen many ways by many people. How we perceive God's assessment of us may be tied to what we think others think of us. Wow, that is a conundrum of major proportions! I am reminded of a brother minister who maintains his next appointment is based on about half what he thinks of himself and half what others think of him. There is substantial wisdom here but in the "long view" it leaves little or no room for God. The quicksand becomes manifest, as we enter our prayer closets for extended periods of time. Then and there the Spirit of the Living God helps us to sift and sort.

Summary And Conclusion

This view is one of coming to terms with the way our Judeo-Christian background has informed our journey. From the inspiration of the psalms to the promises of the one who called himself the Son of Man, and abiding truth emerges. It has a way of explaining both our Lord's first and his second coming. In all cases it has to do with "holiness and godliness." Our hope is encompassed in an eternal love that can give us untold joy, as generations pass. No one is above this view and in one way or another all are ultimately subjected to it. There is a call for celebration not because we emerge as people of hope but as the Holy One reveals himself both as God and man.

All of this leaves us with more open doors than we can possibly enter. It is not lack of opportunity to come to grips with this; it is virtually too much which strains our often impotent powers. The fixing of this understanding to take the "long view" is maybe the most crucial and relevant doctrinal principle that waits to be fully received. Its benefits are too numerous to mention. Perhaps to make the mistake of not wholeheartedly accepting it is akin to splashing in the Pacific Ocean alone, shouting your independence. Today can very well be a brand new beginning because, at last, we have seen the light of his mercy, love, and never-ending powers. Humility of heart and mind should very well carry today and all the tomorrows.

Apostolic Instruction

Introduction

Saint Paul is "on a roll!" He keeps on coming with what he expects of the followers of Christ, as he has nurtured them. It is as though in a breathtaking fashion he wants to be sure his dear people are instructed properly. The words ring with excitement. Today's readers also feel the holy heat that is generated. The words are not theologically demanding as the same found in some of the passages from both Galatians and Romans. The elementary way we can experience the passage is very helpful. In short, it is difficult to misunderstand what is being conveyed. While it might appear a bit simplistic for veteran theologians, it touches the essence of Christian discipleship!

The generous expression, found in easily understood words and phrases, is thrilling to anyone seriously seeking to follow the Christ. We discover so much in so few words and are brought face to face with the contemporary scene and living out the faith. It is class 101 in the exercising of a way of life couched in terms so dynamic even non-believers could get excited about the life we profess! Furthermore, we are given a springboard that encourages and enables us — here and now — to be Christ's people not merely in theory, but in fact. Friends, for the kingdom's sake, this is all very important and helpful. Give thanks for such motivating inspiration.

Focus

We are called to exercise a formula for right living.

Body

1. Commands are required for our well-being.

Like rifle shots, the Pauline teaching comes to us hitting its mark again and again. Do we feel like we are at a remarkable shooting gallery, being hit by blessed requirements? Well, that might be a bit of a stretch for the imagination but it seems to me the point is well taken. Over and over we are pelted by commanding and forceful language. The apostle doesn't want us to get away and run the danger of languishing in fields of indifference. Such fields "miss the mark" and — at best — allow for a temporary respite from the insistence that comes from his teaching. We are privileged people, as the shots hit us and provide spiritual direction!

We are naturally resistant to anything or anyone telling us what we can or cannot do and perhaps think. Many of us take the attitude that since we are being told, we are not going to succumb for any amount of reward! Of course, the beautiful and awe-inspiring part of the passage is "the one who calls you is faithful...." This gives purpose and even glorious sequence to our following orders. We belong to the Lord and he belongs to us. So, why shy away from that which brings us fulfillment under his lordship? Resist long enough and we are going to "backslide," as old-time Methodists would say. Reluctant and belligerent children of the Father create their own problems.

Is there self-interest in all of this? Well, yes, I do believe so. Some of you may be tempted to say "but don't go there." I think it necessary we do that very thing. It is immeasurably inspirational and satisfying in the best sense to "rejoice always, pray without ceasing, and give thanks in all circumstances." It is as though we are enveloped by a teaching much bigger and better than we are. We have tapped into a stream of living water and it really and truly feels good! In reality it is doubtful we do anything completely free from self-interest. Otherwise, we would be sacrificing our personhood, given to us by the Father, and intended to be molded after the one who gave his life for us. Who and what we are is at stake and that is preciously powerful.

Are we dealing with indoctrination? If we are, it seems to me we have to label it "necessary and vital." In a sense, the faith is transmitted by indoctrination that includes commands in addition to the Ten Commandments. Saint Paul is a great teacher and his rabbinical skills show in his writings. In a magnificent way such requirements are given birth by a spiritual dynamic that propels them into our midst for consideration! His people are already a part of God's kingdom. What they need now is "apostolic instruction" to carry them forward. It is training that is "basic" and promises more than the world can ever give. While they may never have noticed it, they were very privileged to have been taught by a brilliant practitioner of the ancient faith.

2. In capsule form we are given the ingredients for successful living.

The birth of a single baby boy launches a more complete way of living out our lives. In a way, we discover an evolution of vast and permanent proportions is taking place. This Jewish child, who became immersed in a Judaism of truly fascinating value, "fulfills the Law." It is a complicated relationship with those who cling to Moses and the prophets and yet the reality is quite simple. We are called through Christ's revelation to live in a certain way and that can — for the most part — be put in a capsule. In some respects, it is almost like holding these priceless gems in our hands and gazing upon them.

To my knowledge, American culture has always said we are born to be successful. It is even maintained that the Puritans thought anyone who wasn't a success was either lazy or sinful! Of course, we have definitely tended to see and measure success in monetary or other material ways. This very strong part of our psyche has led to some living that has not only been unhappy, but even disastrous. Failure after failure can be seen for anyone to observe. This is not judgmental; it is a way of knowing people by their fruits. One of our monumental problems in America is having the strength and fortitude to unlearn what we have been taught about success. It appears we have been inflicted by a persistent ailment: You must succeed "the American way" or indeed you have failed.

The apostle maintains "this is the will of God in Christ Jesus for you." So, in a pointed way he seeks to convey the road to living that is successful. It transcends the common and well-worn path of a secular world that aids and abets misery born of a misunderstanding. The ages and our history speak often, and sometimes in picturesque ways, of the tragedy of turning one's back on a few words geared to set us straight with the Father. Is there any doubt in human sin and the desperate need of a Savior? Isn't it shockingly amazing the way even professing Christians have refused to follow such a simple and practical teaching? How can humankind be so stupid? Yet, but for the grace of God there go you and I!

Those men and women who cook, know about ingredients. Mess up a little and you can have something indescribable. Mess up a lot and you run the risk of total embarrassment. It is likewise true in our spiritual lives, as we seek to be successful in God's sight. The Christian life requires flesh-and-blood living. Anything less reduces it to propositions that give enjoyable moments of mental gymnastics but little in pulsating behavior that elevates the Christ. There is an enormous and crucial difference between Christianity that stops in attitude with Good Friday and one that celebrates the Resurrection and all that follows. Our dear Lord is the chef and Saint Paul is the waiter. Taste and see that is good!

3. It is in the give and take of living that saints are born.

During my doctoral program, a special and lasting lesson was learned. Simply stated: Preachers must be in touch with the living concerns of their parishioners in order to be effective. The finest homiletical and theological works of art will fall on deaf ears, unless such concerns are addressed. Paul must have been an expert at correcting this! By his own admission, he was not much of an orator and hardly an average speaker. What he did understand was the necessity of being in touch with the overt and latent pressing interests of his people. He knows firsthand how saints were born.

Take out spiritual formation and discipleship and what do we have? Well, if our emphasis is the academic and theoretical, most likely we produce people who are stunted in their spiritual growth. Flesh and blood participation, yes, and immersion in people's lives — in time — mean so much to others. Granted, there must be a balance to our ministries, but let us never skirt the issue of the joys and sorrows of humankind, as lived day-by-day. The text is very clear about practicality in the parish and beyond. Some preaching is geared toward excellence in a narrow professional sense. We must be professional but always being sure we are assisting our people in their lives, so they can become more like Jesus the Christ. We preach to and for others, not merely to impress in wrong ways.

"Saints" was a rather common term in the ancient church. To live as the apostle suggests and requires, a lofty level of living those outside of the faith could hardly miss. "Giving thanks in all circumstances" was something most unique in a world of rudeness and crudeness. Someone must be out of his/her mind to live that way! Of course, how many people do you know who would agree with the ancients? My guess is that a very large number of people would insist on the sheer impracticality of it. It's a fine idea but it won't work in a real honest-to-goodness world. We serious-minded Christians have been in that bind for years. The world tells us in many ways that we should provide instruction that will work.

Like Advent, Paul's teaching is intended to be in preparation for the coming of the Lord. We are to be "blameless at the coming of our Lord." Whether we are looking to the first or second arrival of this God/man, our calling is to be in a period of preparing to greet him on bended knees. We have anticipated him and our readiness for the event will be manifest to the Savior of humankind. If it is the manger scene, our task is clear. If it is his appearing in the clouds, our task is also quite clear. Don't be caught unprepared! The utmost seriousness of this cannot be underestimated. However, by way of a precaution, we are counseled to "test everything." Remember, when he did not return in the first century, some Christians were caught off guard.

4. The beautiful spiritual life can be awesomely simple.

The Amish people are both striking and remarkable. This is especially evident among the "old order" group. Having served churches in northern Indiana, their presence was often a joy to me. The horses and buggies sometimes seemed to inundate the countrysides. The plainness of their attire was an inspiration to many of us. It wasn't that they were without problems. In fact, some of their youth from time to time were singled out for their rowdiness and intemperate drinking. However, the overall impression certainly seemed positive. Few people poked fun at them and many admired them. Along with Paul, their priorities were clear.

The call to us is not to be anti-intellectual and irrational. It is one that bulldozes away the debris of impractical theology that tends either to appeal to the ego only or a certain onesideness, freezing out the easy to understand. Granted, there may be those who find this a veiled attempt to put down time-honored theological education. That in no shape or form is my purpose. Falling in love with the finer points of in-depth study of religious doctrines is not inherently evil. But if that is all there is to one's life, the problems of genuine Christian practice can become colossal. After all, a simpleton can be just a simpleton and reflect little or no understanding of Pauline teaching! There is always the dilemma of leaning too far in any direction.

Untold numbers grew up on the pithy saying "Jesus loves me this I know for the Bible tells me so." While many of us smile at the rudimentary nature of these words, there is a mysterious way in which they provide both an entrée and closing to our lives. Indeed, spiritual living at the highest levels can be both awesome and simple at the same time. In parishes across our land there are those devoted Christian soldiers who know little beyond the necessities of which Paul speaks but they do them. They also know what it is to experience them at work! Is this a means of elevating uninformed and misinformed souls who mean well? Quite the contrary, it is a way of accepting Jesus' invitation to be like children.

There is a radiance to some people, isn't there? Their faces glow. Their eyes are bright. Their smile is infectious. Their gait is noticeably confident. Perhaps there are not as many as we would like, but they are among us. We only have to be alert, sensitive, and observant. The magnificence of the apostolic instruction before us really calls us to newer depths of behavior, built upon profound understanding of the gospel witness. The preciousness, vitality, and wholesomeness are there for all to see. Such people do not set out to impress anyone, especially their Lord! It is with the abiding of the Holy Spirit that their gift is presented to be appreciated and imitated. There is such a naturalness to all of this it can escape our full attentions. May God forbid!

Summary And Conclusion

To share and absorb one of the most colorful and yet profound passages in Holy Scripture is a blessing in numerous ways. The various opportunities for good it spontaneously created give us a peek into the unlimited storehouse of the blessed Lord. The formula is there. It is not the entirety of the gospel message but it is imperative to an abundant life here and now. Can it be this has escaped vast multitudes, even in the churches? I strongly suspect the answer has to be in the affirmative. The numerous one-syllable words that come to us greet us much like prized roses in a garden filled with many varieties of flowers that are attractive but at a closer look are mostly lackluster.

Saint Paul places his lesson, leading to victorious living, squarely before us. To every age his challenging invitation bids us to accept and practice ideas emerging from his relationship with Jesus the Christ. By now, some of us are probably saying to one another by look and/or word, let's give it a try. He is like that in most of his writings — and in effect — is proclaiming, "Well, come on let's get with the program." Even as this highly motivating message is considered, we dare not miss the concluding part of the text. Recall, "May the God of peace himself sanctify you entirely." He is well aware of the goal present and the fruition of practicing what he preaches. Try it, you will like it, now and forevermore. Our spirit, soul, and body are to be kept sound. Amen.

Secret Revealed

Introduction

At last it happens! Jesus the Christ is born of a woman and is here for all to see in flesh and blood. Paul, as is often the case, is in a celebrative mood. It is as though all of creation is pulsating with his entrance into history.

Human nature has a way of enjoying secrets and naturally wants exposures to occur. We are fascinated by the possibility of something or someone being revealed. In this case it is far more than fascinating. It is thrilling beyond adequate words to depict. History seems to stop!

Our faith is deeply enriched by accepting and believing the revealed secret is for all of humankind. While it is "my gospel," as the apostle says, it is also a universal and one-of-a-kind happening that he simply attests to. But we would be impoverished without his special touch.

His words are heavily freighted in a brilliantly cast look into what God the Father had finally decided to do. It is not just a prayerful affirmation. It is a theological gem that says so much so quickly we can be caught off balance. Of course, Romans is known for that and this passage especially calls for our complete attention and study.

Focus

God's Son visibly comes on the stage of history.

Body

1. What was shrouded in holy secrecy becomes evident.

God has a way of doing these things to us, doesn't he? By this is meant, of course, not in the same magnitude as our Lord's coming but in our own personal and professional lives. For example, some of us may have learned more about ourselves and others after sixty years of age than before. Some of our questing and inquiries of a lifetime find us with answers and explanations hitherto unknown. Sometimes we discover that what we wanted to know is simply not available to us, until we have lived many years. Sometimes the surprises are so wonderful and at other times far less than wonderful! All in all, this is God's doing.

Had God been keeping something or someone from us in this holy secrecy? Well, yes, I guess so. After all, who has all of the answers here and now and forever and ever? It isn't you and me. Our experience and formal education, regardless of its quality and quantity, are never enough to make us reliable experts on much of anything. We may act like that is not true and parade our resumes across the Internet for all to admire. The reality is if the Creator of the universe and the Father of our Savior and Lord wants to keep a secret, there is nothing we can do about it! Therein lies our security and peace, as we humbly acknowledge his greatness and our littleness.

Dare we talk about or perhaps even debate the timing of the event? As we understand history, we might very well conclude the coming of Jesus and his ministry should have happened in some other generation or century. Is that blatant arrogance? I don't think so, as long as we admit our views are always severely limited and our understandings less than perfect. Frankly, I think it is healthy to theorize about other periods in history for his entrance, as long as we are willing to admit to what we are doing. Whoever became any less by testing revelation in a way that can cause us to refine our faith? Such struggles under the lordship of Christ are therapeutic and can be delightfully helpful.

The weaknesses and, I dare say, the sins of all humanity allow us to stand just so much in the ongoing and colossal conflicts of the world. If God gave us more than we could bear, he would be untrue to his word to us. Therefore, his refusal to make manifest to us people, places, and things that will strongly influence our destiny is necessary to his providential care. This is truly a safeguard for all his children — past, present, and future. We should be on our knees thanking him for omniscience solely found in the Creator of all. Have we forgotten? God does not make mistakes and with that as a part of our basic thought patterns, we are equipped to conquer all under the powers of the Holy Spirit. Failure to believe this sets us up for human errors and perhaps a lasting pattern of disappointments.

2. An extraordinary person at a particular time in history was born among us.

The Judeo-Christian tradition had already witnessed the likes of Noah, Abraham, Moses, and David. Who could ever possibly forget their genius and contributions to all of us? Then, to broaden our perspectives, we discover such luminaries as Socrates, Buddha, Confucius, and Mohammed. Mysteries and miracles surround all of them. To debate who is right or wrong becomes mostly irrelevant, largely because their impact on world history is well known. Some can and do make a case for their entry on the world scene being something of a "Christ event." Of course, much of this is well beyond our puny minds to comprehend.

There are any number of people, especially reputable scholars, who would draw comparisons. They would include Jesus in a pantheon and find him just one among several. On an intellectual level among those who seek to know world religions and philosophies in an objective sense, this seems to work very well. For those of us — including some of the intellectuals — our values in a personal Savior and Lord come to the forefront and may very well collide unceremoniously. To know Jesus as a person who continually is present in one's life means differing from others who can be what they are, with certain lines drawn. This interaction is increasingly true in our lives.

Is it tenable or even possible to absolutize, so to speak, our loyalty to the babe born in Bethlehem? This is invariably present as a problem for Christians. Yet, as those of us deeply involved in ecumenism over the years know, there is a practical answer. The search for Christian unity is just what it says it is. The focus is on Christ who wants all of us to be one. Beyond that clear understanding is the imperative of interreligious dialogue. We can do both! In fact, I do believe, we must do both. The complicated world in which we live will tolerate little else. Realistically, our "head in the sand" approach can make us virtually irrelevant to untold numbers. We proceed with such an approach, inviting perilous times.

Who are we to say our "holy secret" provides us with a monopoly on God's wisdom? Are we privy to all of God's secrets? Having stated those inquiries, I would not want to belittle in any way the revelation we have most assuredly received. The followers of Jesus, born of Mary, are special people that want to share their faith. If this creates arguments and even conflict, so be it. To do less is to deny the very extraordinary person to whom we have vowed allegiance. Faith and works come into play. We see if there is faith, then there must be works and that means some form(s) of witnessing. Hopefully, we also see that legitimate works are born of genuine faith. It is a distinct privilege to be a disciple of the "Lamb of God, who takes away the sins of the world."

3. What God's people had been yearning to see becomes reality.

We can only imagine in faith the yearning that had taken place through centuries for the Messiah. Judaism always had a faithful remnant that was sensitive to God's promise of someone who would come and save his people. We see this especially in the prophets with Isaiah standing out. Their faithfulness generation after generation, as they waited, is certainly one of the brightest lights in all of the history of religions. Some charismatic personage would come on the scene and even do wonders for a time. It wasn't long, however, until it was evident their Messiah had not arrived. But the Jews were tough people who refused to give up, so it eventually happened.

They didn't know and probably didn't even suspect he would also be made known to non-Jews. The apostle tells us "made known to all the Gentiles." Then, he wants his Jewish brothers and sisters to know this is "according to the command of eternal God." It is a way of conveying to them that they should not look for another. Jesus the Christ was there among them. He was preaching, teaching, and healing. At times he performed miracles and the firmly entrenched Jewish hierarchy had to deal with it. Reality of messiahship was all about them but relatively few of his people believed. Then, the Gentiles are invited and guess what? They began to be believers and followers in the millions.

This is so like God, isn't it? The way is being prepared and finally is concluded with John the Baptist. The Jews had long been hungry and thirsty for their fulfillment to an already great religion. After all, didn't Jesus say quite directly that he came to "fulfill and not destroy" the Law? It is like a momentous evolutionary force was set in motion after the fall of man and is now completing its mission. Was Jesus a revolutionary? Yes, in a way, but Holy Scripture brings us a message of evolution, also. He carried with him in his teaching and behavior characteristics not unlike what they had for many, many years. So, at the end of the preparation Mary gives birth to her baby, who in most ways is a natural result of all that had gone on before.

We must never be too hard on our Jewish friends. For, after all, haven't we been guilty of refusing to see and accept the reality of our spiritual lives? Admittedly, our lack of vision may not at all be at the level of their blindness but let us not brag about our superiority. My Jewish colleagues tell me that "triumphalism" angers them more than anything else about Christians. We have seen the light and they haven't! We received, as Gentiles, the revelation secondarily. To put this matter in perspective it helps to read and ponder Romans 9, 10, and 11. While Paul must have had many enemies among his countrymen who hated him, he never gave up hope for them. Salvation is originally from the Jews and not the Gentiles. Who better to spread the gospel than a former Jewish rabbi?

4. God leaves no doubt that he has acted in a singular fashion.

The words "according to the command of eternal God" have a way of telling us this is the way it is. The will of the one and only true God, the Father of our Savior and Lord, has been done for all to see and make response. We are to have no doubt about the coming of

Jesus, born of the Virgin Mary, among us. Some would label this the Almighty's unilateral action. Christians of all persuasions know this to be true and bet their lives and deaths on it. It is a sobering and awesome declaration. If you are looking for someone else, forget it. If you want to continue to expect a future Messiah, don't waste your time and energy.

The Lord God of the universe has spoken now and forevermore. Mary's son is the one, the only one Christians are called to follow. Others, such as Peter, James, John, and Paul, will provide guideposts through their witness and writings, but this Jewish baby boy is the one who provides salvation. Through him comes forgiveness of our sins. Our repentance that is made to anyone or anything else will not fall on inconsequential ground. What is needed to be brought into full view has happened. No more wandering for those waiting for the ultimate to appear. He is among us and the heavens shout their approval. Praises be to God the Father for his Son, Jesus the Christ! For those of us living it is a preeminent privilege to know the event happened once and for all.

The "only wise God" reveals his secret at precisely the right moment he has chosen. It is not one of generalities but one of the decidedly particular. All wisdom that matters resides in him and is dispensed as he deems fit. What greater security can there be? We have hope in someone far bigger and better than ourselves. Those who seriously follow Christ have a peace that does surpass all understanding. It is not as the world gives. Its peace evaporates in both good and bad times. Our peace remains steadfast, as long as we cling to him and carry our crosses in victory. What the world calls wisdom must fall by the wayside. It must never be allowed to set our priorities or get in the way of serving the one, the only one.

The foundation is firmly in place and sinners, both Jews and Gentiles, are beckoned to come and believe. They are also inspired to turn their faith into action and make love a vital and healing energy for all to observe. Will there be other secrets and mysteries? Of course, the answer is an uncomplicated, "Yes." Our incompleteness will not go away, because as yet, we are not what we are intended to be. Full perfection eludes us. Nevertheless, to be convinced we are on the right road to eternal glory is enough. What more can humankind ask? Think of the millions over the centuries who wanted — sometimes in agony — what you and I have. What shall we do with so great a salvation? Our answer should be just as clear as God's explicit revelation.

Summary And Conclusion

The culmination of ages of yearning is now at hand. The great and often unfathomable streams of human experience and God's omnipotence seem to come to a unique intersection in time and space. The forces and energies of all that "was, is, and shall be" have brought to humankind the gift above all gifts. The Word came and dwelt among us. Considering the day and time, eyewitnesses were many. Let there be no doubt the Savior is on the scene. He comes in flesh and blood. Institutions of that day and time would not be able to defeat him. His body, the church, in its broadest and most diverse forms would continue, victorious even against the gates of hell.

So, the continual challenge is put forth to humankind. The secret has been revealed. Will you receive him as your Savior and Lord? To reject Mary's son is not to prevent him from knocking at the door of your heart. The invitation will go on unabated, at least, in this life. The magnitude of this divine enticement to come and live as a new being continues, at times, to enthrall even the most hard-hearted souls. Their rejection stands side by side with the Father's Son wooing them. And, at times, they blow their cover and are on the verge of accepting him, only to return to their former selves whimpering, "Not yet." What shall we do with him? The word is out and has been for 2,000 years. The Lord calls and death comes. We are intended to live for him and spend eternity with him.

Training For A Purpose

Introduction

Some years ago, many of us, like others before and after, went through basic training or boot camp. It was a time to get thoroughly acquainted, usually with either the army or navy. It was also a time of endurance. The hardened and veteran men of years' experience sought to teach us the elementary principles of living in the military. The "old salts" in the navy used to delight in bringing us down several notches. This was their method of clearing away obstructions to the teaching they were providing. Was it fun? Not really. Did funny things happen to us? Well, yes and some were embarrassed to tears. Some could barely contain their anger.

What I remember most about my boot camp was the closeness I felt to the living God. Truth was, I didn't have anyone else that would listen in compassion to my groans of awkwardness and reluctance to give up a comfort zone. At Christmas time we were given liberty to be with our families. With little hair and a face somewhat scarred because of a straight razor, my appearance was not that of a wise and proud public school teacher. In retrospect, it was one of the best times with my family I had ever had. Their son, grandson, and brother was in training. His, and their, Savior — Jesus Christ — was present in a new way. It was as though he had been reborn among us.

Focus

We are trained in order to be useful to others.

43

Body

1. A negative individualism is counterproductive.

When Christ was born among us, he began early on to have apostles close to him. While they were strong individualists, not one was allowed to go it alone and be the only spokesperson for our Lord. Even Peter, who seems to be dominant in the gospels, is not allowed to tell the others what to do. And when we visit with our Catholic friends, we discover — for the most part — the holy father in Rome is held in high esteem but is not experienced as a leader who "lords" it over them. As we study Catholicism we see checks and balances in the Vatican that do away with negative individualism.

As we read the New Testament, there is the witness of the four gospels. Even the synoptic gospels show some differences among them. Then, John comes along and thrills us with both mystery and mysticism! However, when we read and study them together, what a magnificent narrative we receive. We are not disciples of Matthew, Mark, Luke, or John. We are disciples of the babe in Bethlehem, born to bring us the good news that is always more than a single individual, except Jesus the Christ. Our training is not allowed to become negative under a single point of view. Christ "gave himself for us that he might redeem us" and that is the most powerful idea humankind has ever heard. Praises be to the Father for sending his Son among us!

There are those who believe they have a "corner on the market" and seek to absolutize the entire religious experience by sectarian teaching and training. Witness the numerous evangelists and revivalists who have "converted" people to their way of thinking. Sometimes their narrowness only becomes apparent years later, as followers cling to disciplines more inflicted upon them than given to them. Our history is filled with examples of those who allowed their egotism and perhaps self-righteousness to get in the way of the true training of Jesus the Christ. So often it seems those who begin with purity of motivation, sooner or later, are overcome by self-importance. Not only is this negative, it is very sad. We are first of all trained to serve the Christ!

44

If we seek continually "to go it alone," how can we possibly witness in helpful ways? The point is not to negate personal evangelism; it is simply to point out the pitfalls of one who loses contact with others, who are just as much committed or perhaps more so. Christ persists in purifying "for himself a people of his own." Highly individualistic models of discipleship tell me the plural "people" may be considered of secondary importance. To be sure, the babe in Bethlehem calls us as individuals but we are parts of the whole and not the whole! Creativity and innovations can be wonderfully valuable gifts for Christ's holy church. They can also be ways for precious human beings to be misled in directions that produce questionable fruit.

2. A singleness of purpose leaves no doubts.

The reason for our training is to make of us people "who are jealous for good deeds." Salvation has come in the person of Mary's son and is intended to be spread among the lives we touch. We are not lethargic people. We are zealous people! Our good deeds are given birth by a right relation with God the Father through his Son, Jesus the Christ. There is excitement and love in all of this that lays before the world, acts of kindness for the spiritual benefit of everyone. No one should be confused by our lives, as we go about being empowered by the Spirit of the holy God. Nonbelievers are to view in their midst actions and even reactions by those redeemed.

There will be criticism for those of us who go about practicing our faith, usually by calling into question our motivations. This is unavoidable and to be anticipated. Nevertheless, in time, doubts will be diminished as the world sees consistency and persistency in our talk and attitudes. Then, the reality of Christ coming can be seen because there are those in flesh and blood who practice his teaching. The birth of the Savior of the world is seen as more than Christmas presents and carols for once-or-twice-each-year Christians. One of the great victories in our pilgrimages is to experience those critics who finally are willing to accept the generosity of God in our lives. The training has gone well and victorious people learn anew that the awesome everyday power of committed Christians is among us.

To win at anything requires concentration. This is certainly true with our walk with the Lord. We cannot be wandering here and there, indecisive about our gift of salvation. Not only did God's Son come to us centuries ago, he has come into our lives and is a living, vibrant presence at this very moment. We are neither to veer to the left nor to the right. We are to walk the straight and narrow pathway that eventually leads to eternity with our blessed Lord. We are in the harness, so to speak, like any race horse who strains down the track to receive the reward. Some of us know what it is to take our eyes off the prize and lose ground in the most crucial race of all. Sometimes it is devastating.

Congregations and pastors should always move forward together. Internal and external unity is decisive in our quest to show the world that Christ has — in fact — come into our lives. The truly spiritually successful bodies of believers are united and move like a mighty dynamo throughout their communities and beyond. Why? Largely because there is no question about the direction they are moving. Even those who never enter a church building have good things to say. A dysfunctional church is never a positive sight. It conveys quickly the fact that those folks are not together and cannot seem to settle on a clear purpose for being. Their deeds in the community cause confusion. If we are ever at fault for such a situation, may God be merciful! We do not want to be the cause of Christ's sorrowful tears.

3. A ministry to others under the inspiration of the Holy Spirit validates itself.

Serving others is articulated by numerous clichés. Obviously, it is part of the air we breathe. Think of the service clubs, such as Rotary and Kiwanis, who promote and practice serving others. They use the same carefully worded phrases that communicate to the faithful that it is very important to put others above yourself. Is this the work of the Holy Spirit? My own experiences and perceptions are affirming because the Spirit flows where it flows. Strange as it may sound, these clubs and those similar in nature are a training ground. Good deeds are all about! In a way, the invisible church, the one without steeples and pulpits, is hard at work.

Solid and genuine ministry, wherever it takes place, has a way of validating itself. The quality is there and manifest to anyone with serious interest. Our lives are to be lived as "self-controlled, upright, and godly" and that can happen in any set of circumstances. The secular and sacred have their boundaries blurred. It is hard to tell one from the other. The Spirit of the living God will not be denied. Christ was born into this world so that others who follow him will look after their fellow men and women. To accept life and live it in that fashion means Christmas is always with us. Why? Because the gifts of serving others are continually being bestowed upon humankind. So, be alert. There are a lot of really good deeds all about you.

Believe it or not, the world and Christians have need for a sign that calls attention to happenings truly benefiting others. Enough of this theoretical stuff; we want that which is real and evidences gems of legitimacy. It seems we all go through periods in our lives that are filled with spiritual mediocrity or worse. We desperately need a sign that shows God still cares about us and ministers through us. When this happens, what a great day it is! All at once what appeared so average or even sub par comes to life and we are thoroughly reminded God has not abandoned us. The validation for which we were looking virtually stuns our senses and thought categories. Christmas wrappings and the gifts contained therein go together in cohesive beauty.

Being zealous in the right ways is a pure work of art to watch. Demagoguery doesn't rear its ugly head. Our works are free from egotistical yearnings. Our love is for more than a bit of kindness. Our motivations are pure and undefiled. Aggressiveness and helpfulness do not collide in bitter disagreement. We know who and what we are. The babe in Bethlehem is elevated for all to see how beautiful it is! Now it can be said and felt that those Christians have something I don't have and I want it! The stars in the heavens sing out in perfect harmony that Jesus Christ is born, and that everlasting love, as practiced in human relations, is possible because we witness it in action.

4. A wholesome sense of service is among those few essentials of the faith.

The long and short of it is we are intended to be useful to and for others in the highest and best sense. Jesus did not just come to us to be adored in a manger. He came to you and me that we might have life and have it abundantly. His promises are a sterling part of the revealed gospel. To sit by the hour and marvel by the hour at an exquisite crèche may be inspirational for us but whom else does this benefit? To laud to the heavens pictures — even icons — of the blessed Virgin and Jesus weeping, is marvelous for us, but for whom else? The grandeur of striking architecture thrills us beyond words. Frankly, what does it do for your neighbor with cancer?

It usually takes the common and human touch to strike a chord in those who are needy and perhaps on the verge of self-destruction. I believe we frequently underestimate ourselves here. The quiet pat on the back sometimes works wonders. No amount of money could have bought the positive sensation. Whisperings of appreciation with deep emotion can send many devils in hell running. Yes, there is a wholesomeness that is essential for anything significant to happen. Praises be to God, the Father of our Lord and Savior Jesus Christ, simple kindness with sensitivity to the Holy Spirit can carry the day! The world yearns — sometimes in agony — for just these simple but very powerful good works.

Christ keeps on asking us, just as Peter, if we love him. If our answer is in the affirmative, we are to feed and tend his sheep and lambs. Through this endeavor we act as vehicles or channels of "bringing salvation to all." Isn't this what we are always to be about? Indeed, how else can we justify our existence as those professing the name of Jesus the Christ? Funny how we keep evading and avoiding that which is of the essence of our being in Christ, as Saint Paul put it. Loving others in a sincere and wholesome way, bears fruit in ways people can view. The Spirit will seek to guide them to accept and understand that this is why Jesus was born among us.

Are we able to enter the "pearly gates" without taking others with us? That question has been posed numerous times. Frankly, I believe it is possible but highly improbable. Why? Largely because it tends to contradict our vocation as Christians. Of course, if we are not formed after Christ's likeness and only play at religion for our own benefit, it is common sense we are going to fail spiritually. Without being judgmental, take an objective look at yourself. What do you see? Better continue to look some more and with intensity. In order to help Christ, we must continually give him away in thoughts, words, and actions. Believe me, the ages prove there is more than enough of him to go around! Stretching beyond these poor and weak spiritual muscles of ours, nevertheless, is to aid and assist our precious brothers and sisters.

Summary And Conclusion

Our dear Lord's coming throws into operation the possibility and probability of good deeds unlimited. His birth has made the difference between the ongoing and pagan understanding of existence and another way of living, replete with precious persons giving themselves in the name of Christ. The pragmatic and useful characteristics of our ministries, lay and clergy, are evidence his coming was and is not in vain. His birth shattered the assumption that life, even for morally upright people, had to be lived stoically with bravery. This is not to discount those religious beacons coming before him. It is to emphasize that his coming brought us a whole new dimension, namely, love in action freely doing good deeds.

So, the "grace of God has appeared" in the person of a Jewish baby boy. In accepting him as personal Savior and Lord with renunciation of "impiety and worldly passions" we are born anew for the benefit of others. Lives that are "self-controlled, upright, and godly" bring to the world a magnificent and yet practical way of serving humankind. The question is: Do you and I believe this? If we don't, why not? The revelation of his salvation to us should not only stagger us with its uniqueness, but empower us to take upon ourselves as many crosses as are laid upon us and be thankful! The call is for a decisive decision to discipleship that upon being fully accepted — leads to untold riches for others. Indeed, how shall we escape if we neglect so great a salvation?

Precious And
Privileged Children

Introduction

The remarkable world of children has always fascinated me. Their naturalness and innocence — in particular — thrills me and serves as a reminder of the intended relationship between us and our Father. Even more, when they are pouty and sometimes destructive, there is a genuineness about them that is so winsome.

Regardless of our attainments, we never seem to rise above the fact we are simply the Father's boys and girls. The great and the less than great are called to admit to this eternal verity, in time. The famous and infamous, sooner or later, understand in some intuitive way their perpetual childhood.

Some of us wish we could experience more childlikeness in our churches and less childishness. There is a huge difference. One is ready for orders from the Almighty. The other complains the orders received are inappropriate or worse! Childlike congregations and pastors are always learning and growing.

Our destinies are tied to being precious and privileged children. The Father's love is always accessible and it always works in perfect harmony with his crucified and resurrected Son. We have so much for which to be grateful! Kneel some place this day and pour out your heart in thanksgiving for your special place and relationship.

Focus

Our dependency on God is the key to our success.

51

Body

1. The Father wants us to imitate his Son.

He "has sent the Spirit of his Son into our hearts...." That simply and unalterably means we are to be like Jesus, as nearly as we can. Through our joys and sorrows we are to remain steadfast in seeking to practice the teachings given to us. Through our good times and bad times we are to stay close. Through our successes and failures we are to hold up mirrors now and then to test our faithfulness to the highest and best we know. There is always another virtue or attitude for which to strive. We like to think in terms of attainment and soon admit we are only going to improve, humbly conceding our incompleteness.

Imitating a person you highly respect may be the most flattering action to the man or woman you have chosen. In Jesus' case it is more — much more — than a lofty level of respect. It is seeking to become like one who came to us as God in the flesh. This is a lot more than trying to become like a Michael Jordan, Barry Bonds, Ronald Reagan, Hillary Clinton, or even Billy Graham! Models of people in our midst and people long gone may be helpful, but they do not have the substance of our Lord and Savior, Jesus the Christ. Even denominations have to be careful that Martin Luther, John Calvin, and John Wesley are not placed ahead of Christ. They are not the source but merely offer commentaries in print and behavior. We are to remember who the priority is.

Perhaps the greatest teaching devotional is the *Imitation of Christ* by Thomas à Kempis. The centuries of readers bear witness to the profundity of this book. In my own experience, I find it second only to the Holy Scriptures. Page after page, in dialogue form, the author drives home the truth that we are to be like Jesus and we do so by being childlike. Who can even estimate the good that has come from this publication, which has been through countless editions? Protestant, Catholic, and Orthodox all benefit. It is more than a rare book; it is inspirational and instructional beyond anything, other than our Bibles. Its thrust is invariably the same as disciple and Christ visit: We are to imitate our Master and Friend.

World history has been influenced and perhaps shaped by those who have imitated others. Kings, queens, presidents, popes, prime ministers, ayatollahs, writers, artists, and scientists all learned from those they sought to imitate. On the more down-to-earth side of life, many of us found Harry Emerson Fosdick a homiletician worthy of imitation. In fact, go to any walk of life and we discover this phenomenon at work. Even the Mafia chieftains patterned their evil ways after those already successful in corrupting human lives! The Almighty knew the power of imitation far better than any of us. So, the best — the perfect one — was sent into our midst that we might know the way of spiritually happy life. The New Testament with the Old Testament (Hebrew Scriptures) sets the stage for us.

2. The Father seeks to be our parent.

We are no longer slaves! We are children and eventually we are heirs. The Father's heart pulsates in loving energy to draw us to him in a relationship, both meaningful and everlasting. Christmas is the beginning of this love story and it continues to work itself out all our lives. It is the parental approach that wants his offspring to return to their rightful place in the scheme of things. The fall of man is reversed and the opportunity — indeed invitation — to rediscover what was intended to be ours is centered upon a Father's love and the gracious gift of his Son. The fallen kingdom so long in force can now be conquered. Talk about faith, hope, and love!

What does a really good parent do? He looks after his precious children, who are the most privileged in the entire creation. This means and implies many things but probably above all is protection and sustenance. Have we not been given minds to protect us from all adversaries? Have we not been given a vineyard that provides for our welfare? In a different way we are protected by a spiritual heart, given to us by our parent known as "Abba! Father!" Then we are sustained by the many spiritual disciplines, especially prayer and Holy Communion. Our God provided again and again. He is the totally good Father whose loving power and powerful love comes to us now and forever and ever. Hallelujah and amen!

Many older parents are being cared for today by their children and to a lesser extent other relatives or friends. As our population grows older and older, there will be greater need for this. It may take the form of a nursing home and/or assisted living quarters. Regardless of the health care configuration, it is coming and with question marks all up and down the line. Attempt, if you will, to relate this to our heavenly Father who is our parent. We will never have to be responsible for his care, or will we? The heart of God yearns for the children of the world — young, old, or otherwise — to come to him. So, his need for us to come to a shelter that protects from hell needs to be met. Just maybe we can minister to the Almighty and have never felt comfortable with that idea.

Even though the New Testament throughout designates God as the Father or in male-oriented language, this must be tempered by maternal and typically female characteristics present. The mystery involved here, especially in light of some theological controversies, is indeed substantial. We are working through a period of history and culture of immense confusion and disagreement. Hopefully and prayerfully, we will not lose our way and move precious children to a chasm that promises nothing but chaos and lost souls. In these days of questing it is good to be reminded that God comes to us as Father, Son, and Holy Spirit. In a sense, there is a parental relationship here that communicates our imperative need to be in a parental-child mode, always dependent on that for spiritual success.

3. The Father desires we huddle close to him.

To cry to one's Father is a fascinating way to depict our closeness to the everlasting God. Jesus knew more about this than you and I shall ever know. There is an almost indescribable intimacy and at times we are simply at a loss to tell others of God's presence. When pushed to describe this experience, I usually acquiesce into trying to say that I know beyond all doubt he is present. There is a sense that someone far bigger and better than yourself is there. It may be for quite sometime, perhaps minutes or even hours, or it may be only for a brief moment. The treasure is one that neither money nor self-help books can bring about.

His image as a faraway God, maybe perceived in a deistic fashion, does not exist. There is the Spirit of Jesus in our hearts, that glorious Son given to us by the Father through dear and blessed

Mary. Don't you feel sorry for those who never seem to get beyond a distant deity, who neither feels nor handles anything or anyone directly? Some have said the founding fathers of our nation were mostly deists. Frankly, that is debatable. Read the original materials of Franklin, Jefferson, and Washington more carefully. Do not depend on those who want to tell you their feelings and thoughts. Evangelical Christianity, to my knowledge, has always preached that God is very familiar with his children. Only as we persistently reject his gracious invitations do we began to perceive him in an abstract manner. Yes, draw near to God and he will draw near to you.

Some saints could hardly tolerate the pressure of his presence. The light and the heat were so intense it became virtually unbearable. Would that every one of us could have that experience! They had snuggled up so close, they felt encompassed and God-intoxicated. To be drunk with the Spirit of which Saint Paul is speaking is one of ecstasy, elation, and elevation. We learn in a sublime way that our spiritual success is, indeed, brought about by our full dependency. A man was asked why he couldn't stop weeping with joy. He said quickly that he had gotten too close to God and was now receiving the aftermath. Thomas Merton knew about this as he penned his many books. For some saints, every day is Pentecost.

We have all heard at sometime or another that God is closer than our very skins. There isn't much eloquence or theological precision in that but it is a way of delineating a blessed connection like no other. My own spiritual journey has many such highly charged human/divine events in it. That does not automatically make me special in a category not permitted to others. It does make me more and more grateful for salvation history that culminated with Jesus Christ. The ancient church was visited time and again by such phenomenon. There is the search, sometimes excruciating among people today, for intimacy with God. It is more than for reasons of secular ambition. There is a groaning after the ways and will of their maker. They have come to their senses and really want to return to their Father!

4. The Father pursues us in loving understanding.

"The fullness of time had come" and there is no object in looking or waiting for the Jewish Messiah. He has come by way of the virginal conception. Blessed Mary was the channel. In a sense she was the mother of God. The early fathers of the church have said so and with powerful emphasis. This indicates we have moved from slave to child to heir and we are not second-class citizens in the kingdom of God. The eternal love has been manifested in a particular and concrete way no human being can annul or invalidate. We find ourselves in a love that knows no bounds and an understanding of his children totally unique, and the angelic hosts sing with divine joy!

His pursuit never relents, even at a death's door. We have known those who regularly put off the requirements of the Christian life. God remains faithful. So, you thought you got away? Does that sound just too pedestrian and secular? I hope not. Why? Because there is a profound truth here and it will not be cancelled out. It has to do with the innate preciousness and privilege we have. One thing God is not: He is not a liar. We ought to see clearly that God will do whatever he decides to do and with whomever he has chosen. There is a great and undeniable life lesson in all of this. While we are pursued in loving understanding, this does not imply we are with God as one buddy to another. To carry that concept very far leads to perversions and prevarications.

God's patience is a virtue of such profundity we can understand it only darkly. Nevertheless, we do have a glimpse. What father desires to have even the most obstreperous child lost forever? Now, we get even closer to the fatherhood of God whose heart is in it! It makes a difference — a big one — whether or not each of his children sidles up to his side and pleads to be in the arms of the only one who can really care indefinitely. This is so deeply personal and requires we consciously become vulnerable. He has more patience than Job! How much more privileged can we possibly be? Yet, often, and probably most of the time, we hold him at a distance, either totally petrified or fiercely independent.

Most of us understand amazing grace just enough to know God cares about us. We have a bit of trouble with a love that has no boundaries. Then, in our most lucid moments it dawns on us the great God of the universe understands and loves us far beyond our wildest dreams. Some very fine churchgoers that I have known say such moments are far and few between. My belief is this is a problem with human perception. God is as near as we want him to be. There is no scarcity in this love that knows no bounds. There is no limit to his understanding of our lives and loved ones. We must learn to cry out more often, "Abba! Father!" It is a wonderful exercise for our vocal chords. It is the means our heavenly daddy uses to take us in his arms and hold us tightly with a supernatural love.

Summary And Conclusion

Say what we will, those professing Christ find great security, stability, and satisfaction in being the Father's boys and girls. Such dependency has been with us in the Judeo-Christian as long as anyone can recall. "The fullness of time had come" and humankind feels the full weight of God's omnipotence, omniscience, and omnipresence. He gives us our worth and identity, specifically as we relate to his Son — our Savior and Lord. All spiritual successes — in a way — are directly related to this understanding of the Christian faith. Are we precious and privileged? Of course, we are! Men and women over the centuries have attempted to find solace elsewhere. But we are extra-special. We have found more than easing of our discomfort.

So, the message is quite clear. We are called to be sons and daughters in the highest and best sense. This royal invitation is given to us by Jesus the Christ coming among us. Yes, we are given the opportunity to become spiritual royalty. Of course, the decision is ours. Jews and Gentiles have access to the gift above all others. What shall we do with the babe in Bethlehem now among us? Today is the day of salvation not only for you and me. It is such a day for others throughout the world. When in doubt as to how to bring this about, fall on your knees like children. Names and faces will come to you, some you will know and others you will not. Appreciate your lowliness. Christ did! Remember we have "the Spirit of his Son" in our hearts. All things are possible with God.

Deep Calling To Deep

Introduction

Wow, our text is not only challenging, it is a momentous portion of scripture that keeps spreading and giving! The profound theology expressed is in some ways more than we are able to handle. Yet, we are called to make an honest and forthright attempt. A conscientious rendering of the passage is in order that others may, at least, taste such wisdom is our goal.

To be chosen "in Christ before the foundation of the world ..." is both awesome and ominous. It is as though our free will has been suspended and a ring of unpredictability floods our souls. Nevertheless, we must live on and seek to fulfill our destinies. We must also work with the knowledge that there is something very special about us Christians.

While John 3:16 has been quoted for centuries as the quintessential statement of understanding God's relationship to us, it both tends to evade and reduce problems in our salvation history. Saint Paul wants more than it offers and yet is not in any sense wanting to contradict it. He seems never to be frightened by those really big ideas. In fact, he insists on providing explanations that make sense to him and should as well make sense to us. Christ's coming completely changed his life in terms of motivations and goals.

Focus

Probing at deeper levels gives a more complete understanding of our faith.

Body

1. To be too simplistic tends to produce spiritual pygmies.

This is not to infer or imply esoteric information is necessary in order not to wallow and eventually die with simple answers to huge and complicated problems. I believe our dear Lord would say to follow such a road is to shut out the "little ones" he came to save. Having admitted this, we must not be reduced into a Pollyanna that sings optimistically day-after-day whatever will be, will be! Such a practicing of our blessed Lord's faith may not be blasphemous or heretical but it will undoubtedly be minimal. This we must shun and be on our guard against. Our spiritual growth demands we keep moving on, hopefully upward.

As a boy, I remember honest people during the time of testimonials saying exactly the same thing at each and every service. It is not that they were in any sense wicked people. However, surely there could have been some indication of change, showing they had moved deeper with their Lord. As a lad, not even into my teenage years, I observed in respect but vowed I would go deeper, much deeper. This was not seen at the time as an attempt to be better than someone else but to acknowledge the enormity of the field with the ground hardly broken. It was a moment of awakening that was only barely a part of my consciousness at the time.

To be blessed "with every special blessing" conveys to me we are to labor in all times and places, and yes, with whomever we find ourselves. This is the best prevention against becoming spiritual pygmies. If we are to be six-feet tall, why settle for four-feet? Unused potential in the personal spiritual realm is a tragedy here and now and forever and ever. May God forgive us! Such work, of course, is not necessarily the visible kind. It may very well go unseen, only to be revealed on the last day. Many experience their labors in vain, only to learn later, frequently much later, that is not the case. Timing is really God's business because we have so little control over circumstances. More than that, we may not even know what they are!

Studying theology and philosophy among seminary students is always a serious task. It is the hope they wrestle with the profundity of the Christian religion in order to understand it in ways that cut below the surface. In our preaching and calling — in particular — the need is for pastors to be able to field questions and comments made by their parishioners. In a way preaching is group pastoral care every Sunday and at other times to enable the person in the pulpit to provide more than clichés. Seminary education is so important in aiding precious human beings in their spiritual formation. Repetition is essential and yet it can also be deadening. Of course, we are reminded to repeat the Lord's Prayer and the creeds with regularity, knowing their basic place in the deposit from which we all eat and drink.

2. We are called to work out our salvation in fear and trembling.

"We have redemption through his blood" is our assurance but it is also a prodding to a more complete understanding of how our salvation is to be treated. To be redeemed by his blood is no small matter! It is here that the ever-popular power of positive thinking types can be stumped and fail to come to grips with something far more significant than a tool for getting our way. To be afraid and trembling means our very personhood is in some way threatened. To become uneasy and yearn for better days under the banner of a nominal faith is no answer. Of course, we should not treat our salvation as a possession, but as a gift that spiritually forms us.

To be called to become more like Christ is to probe so deeply we not only learn of our crosses, but receive them with gratitude. We carry them and are educated in the ways of the master. The saints testify to the magnificence of these crosses. Their sainthood most likely depended on them carrying such uninviting objects that have truly taken on many forms throughout the ages. What for one was a cross for another was not. What one would have chosen for himself or herself was not the one selected by him. Saints have been known to cry out in gratitude for those burdens that turned out to be loads of love. We have much to learn here! Perhaps we must persist in getting a legitimate definition of sainthood back into our vocabularies.

The birth of Christ flung into motion "the mystery of his will." How can an innocent Jewish baby boy have anything to do with the excruciating and totally uncivil experience of crucifixion? It seems to me this only illustrates the greater the sacrifice of the innocent, the greater the power of that person. The Eucharist or Holy Communion speaks to this. The death of spotless animals could never be enough to atone for the sins of humankind. It took the pure and holy Son of the Father. There is a depth to this that is never fully discovered. Our Catholic and Orthodox friends understand that better than any Protestant I have ever known. To take the Sacrament in the understanding of Christ's "real presence" is to begin to get at these depths of which we are speaking.

A crucifix can speak countless words to the believer. An empty cross speaks of Easter. A crucifix conjures up images of Good Friday and that horrendous death scene. Frankly, we can't have one without the other. The "fear and trembling" of the crucifixion is built into the fabric of our fabulous faith! How else can we "live for the praise of his glory"? Note the ongoing depth of Saint Paul's lengthy passage. We have a crucified/resurrected Lord, who began his journey on this globe at Christmas. The most epochal of all presents is his salvation brought by who and what he was, the Savior of humankind. As we exercise in humility and sincerity our hearts, minds, and souls we begin to scratch the surface of a depth mostly beyond us. Nevertheless, the exercise is indispensable to our well-being.

3. Pleading ignorance in spiritual matters can be disastrous.

In dismay, my discoveries lead me to any number of church people, who appear not to have the slightest notion of the depths of our religion. A once each day devotional is about as far as they get. Even those who are fairly regular in worship attendance can embarrass themselves. Naming the gospels and the golden rule may be about as far as it gets. I am not trying to be unkind. Certainly my purpose is not to be judgmental. My great concern is how can such persons defend our precious faith. It becomes "oh you know" kind of thing.

We all have wide and deep gaps in our knowledge of spiritual matters. We can rightfully excuse ourselves upon occasion. However, to drift along in some dreadful bliss can be a disaster. For example, how can we answer basic questions asked us by inquiring people in search of salvation? When asked about our current passage, what can be intelligently stated without study and pondering? We are supposed to know our Lord in more than the ways taught us in a manner that eventually produces more heat than light! People need answers today and they generally want them from other lay people. The most professional thing a clergy person might do is take all of his/her members through Christianity 101 again, or the initial time for some. We clergy can be seriously at fault for our parishioners not knowing as much about the Bible as Oprah or David Letterman.

The riches of our faith are priceless and cannot be measured in secular terms. The deep waters are there to be explored unhurriedly. Anyone can take difficult passages, after just becoming thoroughly acquainted with Holy Scripture, and be blessed many times over. In view of the fact large numbers of church members have blocks of time and financial resources, we are brought face-to-face with something quite unpleasant. Well, let's go ahead and ask the question. Are we ignorant of large areas of the spiritual life because we want to be? Perhaps it is because we simply — by design — have other priorities more pressing. Since we "were marked with the seal of the promised Holy Spirit," how can any of these inquiries by relevant? May our dear Lord be merciful!

The resolution to our ignorance is mostly found in prayer and study of Holy Scripture with the added ingredient of congregational worship. To take these areas seriously is to banish ignorance in spiritual matters. We are enabled to probe at the deeper levels and begin to enjoy the excitement of what it really means to be a disciple of the Christ. Then Saint Paul's brilliance may not become crystal clear, but at least we are familiar with the magnificent and marvelous theological artistry put before us. Yes, and when we are stumped, we are to go to prayer, not as an escape but as a tool to continue our in-depth excursions. We value the news in-depth. Why can't we do as much for our spiritual lives? It seems to me the choice is plainly before us.

4. Everyone — in a sense — is his/her own theologian.

Ideally, every person who professes Jesus Christ as Savior and Lord is on a theological journey that makes him/her a student of God. It is a beautiful and even sacred phenomenon to observe some laity commit themselves to study the Father, Son, and Holy Spirit. They are never ordained but do they ever look like and act like trained and vibrant clergy! We owe the small group movement a debt of gratitude. Of course, it is not that different from the vital societies given birth in England by John and Charles Wesley. Spiritual sensitivities are brought to the surface. Both personal and group growth is seen. They are "God's own people," who either are or are becoming their own theologians!

Some of our laity will wrestle with passage after passage. They refuse to run away from the noble task of becoming theologically literate. Such men and women have always made me shout for joy! I believe some understand the meaning of being colleagues together better than some clergy, especially those who are turf conscious. We are blessed today with them taking courses in colleges and seminaries, sometimes on a non-credit basis. We clergy can learn from them, provided we are humble and honest. Their voyage takes them into the depths of theological inquiry and understanding. Think how proud the apostle would be! While we have enormous pockets of illiteracy in our flocks, we also have quite the opposite. There are adults determined to call unto the deep.

There are those who would maintain this only leads to private interpretation that can take valued disciples in too many hurtful directions, including toward hell. We do need to admit church history is filled to overflowing with those who go so far as to build entire denominations on a few verses. Such radical movements, I fear, have more to do with egotism and pride than anything else. The absolutism of one or a few can build cages for all those who are willing to agree and adjust accordingly. But let's not be too harsh in our day and time. We have checks and balances today that provide stopgaps for those who are traveling toward a dead end. We are helped greatly by knowing we were marked with the seal of the promised Holy Spirit.

We ought not to frighten our flocks by telling them they are expected to become their own theologians! Pastoral guidance is often necessary and this means clergy who are rooted and grounded in the faith, refusing to be threatened by bright laity. My experience tells me we always have some men and women who know more about certain areas than we do. As hard as it is to admit, that is even true in a spiritual sense. They are willing to dig deeper and will do so! Never underestimate the work of the Holy Spirit in parishes, and any place, for that matter. Secure within their own theological understanding, pastors can lead and enable magnificent blessings to occur among their precious people. At times the dear Lord just prods us to turn them loose!

Summary And Conclusion

The apostle's gift to us in this portion of Holy Scripture provides a cutting edge of growth for many of us. His emphasis is Christological and offers the opportunity for us to kneel and worship our Savior and Lord more completely. In addition, it especially provides a thrilling time of study that makes us forget all about the light-weight stuff we have been reading in popular devotionals! With heart and mind perfectly attuned to the Holy Spirit our labors become more and more fruitful. We are brought in touch with understandings — indeed wisdom — that enable us to celebrate Christmas on a daily basis, recognizing in joy our greatest gift is the Christ.

The challenge to the pastors and key laity in our time is much what it always has been. We are to know about Jesus Christ and accept him in our hearts and minds without reservation. We must not be spiritually starving people, refusing the royalty in our midst. A lazy and unsettled mind is a negative force in our quest to know our Lord. A heart that is barely lukewarm is a major problem — if allowed to continue — because we can never tell where we are going to land in matters of spiritual depth. Often, the Holy Spirit leads some of us to focus on disciplines that will move us into those heavenly lands where untold riches are plentiful. We must move from our glasses of skimmed milk to steaks perfectly cooked and ready for our consumption. Time is passing, so we must be at work.

The Baptism Of Our Lord
Epiphany 1
Ordinary Time 1
Acts 19:1-7

Taking A Necessary Step

Introduction

The closeness between John the Baptist and Jesus can hardly be overemphasized. It was true from the time of their conceptions and the evident, close relationship between their mothers. It is said that in certain parts of the world there are still a few who follow only the baptizer. After 2,000 years the transition apparently has not been made.

Among those disciples that Paul found, they had no clear witness of the far greater one who would follow John. This may very well be a special word for those today who are good, morally upright people but have not made the discovery of Jesus the Christ. Our duty to instruct and inspire is an extraordinary opportunity.

It is likely these twelve or so knew of Jesus and had awesome respect for him. What they apparently did not know was that salvation was found in him and only him. Paul took the situation as he found it and made one of spiritual progress, doing so without denigrating John. Would that all spiritual transitions could be as smooth as this one!

The wise student and teacher attempts to preserve what is good and useful. They seek to improve and make additions with some needed corrections. There was no reason for competition between John and Jesus. That would be counterproductive or worse. The moment was crucial and Paul did not fail.

Focus

What we have may be good but it is only a beginning.

Body

1. We made a good start and then things began to fall apart.

How often this is true for you and me! The Christ is born in us and we begin to experience signs that everything he says is true. It isn't that the baptist is vying for our full attention. Some person, organization, or idea is making a move to loosen the relationship with our Lord. A pastor, who is charismatic and demanding, may become our sole interpreter of the Christian faith. A sectarian group, emphasizing certain points of scripture to the detriment of others, may become our only home base. An idea of genuine worth is allowed to become virtually the only one that guides our lives. The subtleties are numerous.

My experiences over more than four decades of pastoring churches tell me goodness is usually shattered by what Saint James labels the power of the tongue. We are moving in our spiritual lives really well and along comes someone who verbalizes something that becomes a bone of contention. Before you know it, the peace that passes all understanding is not only gone, it is so far removed that the people involved have moved beyond the perimeters of practicing the faith. What happened? Those who have a courageous spirit and real humility begin to retrace their steps. Eventually the discovery is made. Christ was sidestepped. His primary place had become optional and certainly his lowly, forgiving heart had been crushed. The good start had been compromised and a loss of faith was at hand.

"Backsliding" was a fairly common term at one time in our country, especially during revival meetings. The gist was usually the same. A precious person had received Jesus Christ as Savior and Lord. That person had begun to practice the Christian life in ways noticeable to others. Then, something happens and there are about as many reasons as there are people. While this may have little directly to do with John the Baptist, it strongly suggests a falling away of something good and supremely meaningful. We may not especially care for such revivalistic overtones, but the message is clear. We are created and intended for spiritual growth. To be seriously thwarted, regardless of how, becomes a sad state of affairs.

The more sophisticated and ritualistic parts of society are not that much different. A daily early-morning mass is not only avoided but becomes strictly an optional experience of the disciple. In time even regular Sunday mass is put on a take-it-or-leave-it basis. So, after some months the one, holy, catholic, and apostolic church has become mostly just another set of buildings and doctrinal concepts best evaded. May God be merciful! In mainline Protestantism this can be seen by secular politics and power struggles within the churches beginning to dominate good people's will and time. Even clergy begin to question their ordination vows and wonder that perhaps God did not call them after all! It's familiar territory, isn't it? Pray often — yes incessantly — that you will not fall by the wayside.

2. The sufficiency of Christ alone is illustrated.

We are born again to be faithful and forever attentive primarily to one person. We know his name and his way. While all the prophets and seers coming before and after Christ make their contributions, he and he alone brings completeness. True, the church — both visible and invisible — enters the picture but without him it has no real power or relevance. Paul found his way in Jesus Christ the crucified. So, our rebirth is an experience that gives us the reason and format for continuing our lives in a victorious manner. We must move beyond John the Baptist or anyone else who has given meaning to our lives.

Many of our parishioners tend to go through years of their lives never coming to terms with the truth of which we are speaking. It is as though a curtain drops and prevents them from fully receiving their Savior and Lord. It is not that they have no knowledge of him, of course; it is that they have a problem of readiness. Perhaps this is the work of Satan that likes things the way they are. Whatever it is, faithful clergy and laity are responsible for leading others to accept the sufficiency of Christ alone. It may be a bigger and more intricate problem than we are willing to admit. I suspect the best way to tackle this is to confess our sins of omission. We knew the right thing to do but we did not do it. As we are forgiven, let us vow to do better for the sake of the kingdom of God.

For those of us who have spent many years in formal education and have decades of experience, it is humbling to recognize this only has practical meaning as we relate completely to Christ. The Lord Jesus is the centerpiece and from him our lives and deaths are made acceptable to the Father. For some still wandering to find another and better messiah it becomes a heart-rending scene for those looking on. We want desperately to do something about this potentially tragic state of affairs. Have we run the race, only to have left Christ off to the side? In our quest for a secular success, have we been blinded by ambition, greed, and status? These are hard questions but they must be asked and more than once.

Sometimes we see and deeply appreciate the kingship of Christ, only to turn a deaf ear to his lowliness. We shy away from a man who was virtually pulverized by the power structures of his day. Yet we are told we must suffer with him in order to rise with him. The crucifixion must never be seen divorced from the resurrection and vice versa. The twin events illustrate in a realistic and graphic way what it takes to understand such all-pervasive sufficiency. Our acceptance of this truth gives us doctrinal grounding that is good forever and ever. To plead the weakness of humanity can only be a trapdoor that acts as a preventative in receiving his gift of baptism and the Holy Spirit. The gift wants to be given. Shall we go through most of life rejecting it? I humbly pray that will not be the case.

3. So much of life is a rewarding preliminary leading to something or someone better.

This concept takes time to ponder. The truth of it is not likely to come quickly. In honesty, perhaps we all need to live long enough to be able to perceive it and the value. Counting our blessings is one way to begin positive pondering on such a matter. Then, we see the connections of how one set of events leads to another and so on. Those who don't have a sense of growth, of course, will have some problematic times trying to deal with this. In terms of the truth of the text we understand John's baptism of repentance was not wrong. It just didn't go far enough. More — substantially more — was in the offing and it would potentially lead to fulfillment, at least, in this life.

From one valid viewpoint our lives are a series of beginnings and, therefore, endings. As times come and go, our lives are impacted and — to some extent — we impact the times. We were never intended to stalemate and live in little more than a parasitic existence. That is a tragedy! In the Methodist connection we move from church to church. We begin and we end. We move into new parsonages and churches, understanding one ministry is finished and another is beginning. My experience has been one mostly of celebration and a sense of accomplishment. Sometimes there are bumps at both the start and the finish but there has been learning and improvement in most cases. I cannot adequately speak of other polities but trust it is much the same.

As the Holy Spirit abides and provides, the awareness of a rewarding preliminary to something and/or someone else is frequently present. We may not know what or who but with our lives thoroughly in the hands of our Savior and Lord anticipation is in the air. Hopefully, this is a common experience for all brothers and sisters. I always looked forward to new appointments, largely because I knew there would be some truly good people ready to greet me. Not only would they provide a welcome, they would minister with me and — if need be — forgive me. Praises be to the mercies of God who enables this to happen! The ordained ministry is so precious and at times we make it more difficult and complicated than it is. This is because we do not trust fully in the one who called us.

Paul's friends in Ephesus did not appear to be unhappy solely with John's baptism. It took the apostle to point to the fact they were actually living in a preliminary period, awaiting more. He was emissary, teacher, and ordained clergy at the same time! Sometimes you and I are put into places where we fulfill the same functions. A key layperson doesn't know about the spiritual riches available to him or her. How can that person know? He/she needs someone to be put in his/her pathway to reveal the need. That person needs someone for instruction, and finally he/she needs a clergy person to put the three together and provide under the guidance of the Holy Spirit for his/her spiritual welfare. Is this only theory or

71

inadequate discipling? No, it allows the Holy Spirit to work for everyone's benefit.

4. We are to acknowledge our mission as agents of introduction.
The input we can insert in others' lives is an area for close inspection. In short, what can we do even now to foster improvement in our brothers and sisters? What ideas or issues or maybe disciplines can enhance others? Well, let's admit this is a wide and deep area of ministry. For example, how can we be sure we are not simply attempting to influence others with our own pet prejudices? Do we have an agenda that doesn't resemble what Christ has in store for us? Yet, we must not go away or perhaps run frustrated in defeat. Only by staying close to Christ will we have the proper words, thoughts, and feelings. Anything less may cause a hailstorm of ill will brewed and stewed by Satan!

It is prudent to be reminded that the Holy Spirit does not make us timid. Instead, this Spirit fills us with power, love, and self-control. We can enable precious people to take a necessary step to substantially improve their spiritual lives. Timidity and essential humility are not synonymous. To be sure, within our strength we are going to fail in the long run. With the strength given us by God we are going to be successful, at least, in terms of right attitudes. Along the way in our lives these happenings occur again and again. Missed opportunities can be the worst of all admissions as one nears the end of his/her life. In our ministries as agents of introduction we are given what is imperative to say and do. Sometimes this means little planning on our part.

Note what a substantial and qualitative difference Paul made. He was an agent of introduction *par excellence*. An amazing and powerful change took place. Do you and I underestimate ourselves? Maybe a better way to phrase it is: Do we question our relationship with God the Father through Jesus, his Son? Still better, is our problem one of needing spiritual validation? Then, we are in crucial need of an agent to introduce us to the finer points of what it takes to improve our ministries! So, it works both ways and this is a means to instruct us in honesty and humility. Praise God from whom all blessings flow, praise him all creatures here below! Our ministries are so multifaceted and fascinating. Who can say what we will be asked to do or refrain from doing tomorrow?

It has been my philosophy since a college student to try to make the good better. This was partly ambition, pure and simple. It was also the sincere recognition that God still had changes to make in me and I had better listen ... carefully. There is that ominously wholesome craving to be more and better. It likely has nothing to do with money and property. It has a great deal to do with the evolution and improvement of one's personhood. In Christian terms, this means to become more like Christ. After all, isn't that the on-going, absolutely fundamental principle, in our pilgrimage? To become more like him is to become more amenable to being agents of needful introduction by solid implication. So ministry is so obvious we have to work at it to avoid it!

Summary And Conclusion

In a way, taking necessary steps with the Father holding our hands is a simplified description of living the Christian life. At each crucial point in our development there is a step to take. We may find it to our liking. Likewise, we may discover we don't like it at all! Paul's friends had a step to take. Otherwise, they would remain thwarted in what was intended for them. This is so like our lives, isn't it? Hopefully, every step shows forward movement under the banner of Jesus Christ. We may be complimented for our goodness, only to learn it just isn't good enough for the eyes of one who is the only one who ultimately counts.

Dear friends, pause to give thanks for your lives. Do so because you know there is more to learn and celebrate, as you and others change to a greater good. There has to be that hunger in us that seeks to eat more solid meat and fewer potatoes. If we but listen attentively, the dear Lord will come to you directly or send someone to provide an opening for you to take the next step. Plateaus may be nice and comfortable but they are also debilitating. In time, as opportunities come and go, they can so erode that they won't support much of anything that is truly valuable. Don't allow the awful shame of such a predicament claim your place in God's kingdom. Stand tall or fall on your knees, whichever is required, and move forward in the spiritual life Christ intends. You will never lack opportunities. He continues to stand at the door and knock.

Getting It Straight

Introduction

What a colorful figure Paul must have been in flesh and blood! His individuality shows a man who refuses to be dominated by anything. For us to be able to experience his ministry, as he went about, would have been something that would have made an indelible imprint on us.

As he wove his life and ministry into his day and time the enemies were many. This was especially true among his Jewish brothers and sisters. Only by the grace of God was he able to fulfill what he had been called to do. The hatred could be intense and his very life was at stake. Nevertheless, as his letters say, he went about in a thankful mood.

One wonders how the Christian movement could ever have gotten off the ground without him. Much of the New Testament reflects his power, personality, and pen. His churches sometimes were battlegrounds but he stayed the course. He wanted his people to get things straight and gave himself totally to see this happen.

Our calling to the pastorate is much like that. We want our people to get things straight. Perhaps the momentous question that is always before us deals with our willingness to give our all. So much real success deals with exactly that matter, which invariably depends upon a deeply personal decision.

Focus

We cannot live our lives well in fragmentation.

Body

1. No one can indefinitely live a morally fractured life.

Sometimes in high places, especially in politics and religion, we watch in dismay and even disillusionment as our icons crumble. The list is long and there is nothing new, that is, if we survey the history of nations and the world. There is no need to name names. They are frequently in the news. Of course, we must be shrewd and perceptive enough to determine the reliability of the various forms of media. This is not easy. In fact, it can be downright difficult! Our temptation may be to point the finger at someone, who has betrayed some of the most basic criteria for living a healthy life. I believe this is only helpful after we take personal inventory.

We view and often experience morally fractured lives all about us. Appearances mislead us and we can be devastated. Never judge a book by its cover is long-standing and sound advice. To be honest, this state of affairs can also work in an opposite manner. Someone may have allegedly fallen and we learn this is only an allegation and is not provable. People deserve the benefit of the doubt — at least, the first or second time. If we don't like someone, it is easy to find him/her guilty and spread the word with glee. It is a quagmire in today's world. Sometimes we know so much and yet we know so little! We all tend to be morally fractured in some way.

To live one's life personally in one way and publicly quite another, certainly and simply calls for correction. We may like to think fornication and adultery are excusable between two consenting adults. It seems fashionable to seal off one's infidelities to a restricted area and claim they have no bearing on our public and vocational lives. I believe this trend increases our illness as a nation and jeopardizes the general welfare. We are intended to be whole human beings with morality at work in every sector of our precious lives. The dear Lord did not come to save us in fragments, leaving some untouched, especially those of our own choosing. We must be brave and brazen like Saint Paul.

Some say early on in their lives, either directly or indirectly, "This part of my life belongs to the Lord, this part belongs to me." In other words, lordship is denied in certain areas. Again, we must not be too judgmental. We all have the same tendency at work in us. It is as though humankind was born with it. Perhaps it illustrates the affliction of original sin! Such fragmentation always and eventually shows itself. The wounds come to the surface. The unforgiven sins become noticeable. The out and out hypocrisy exudes an odor that hardly anyone can miss. It is a sad and very trying time. Of course, the remedy is found in repentance and forgiveness with the promise to live a new life. Then, all aspects of our coming, going, and staying show wholeness. The world, believe it or not, is always looking for just such a person.

2. We are called to live in Christ as a distinctive human being.

To live in him is to be formed by him and that is not to make everyone look, more or less, exactly the same. To get things straight means we become human beings who stand out in the Lord. Yes, the body has many parts, and each of us is a special part. More in Pauline language, our bodies are temples of the Holy Spirit. Think what a magnificent quilt we are throughout the world! There are too many shades and sizes to count. We were all bought with a price and that adds immensely to our image. Christ died and arose for us. Now, we die and arise with him. We are a witness to the world.

Billions of dollars are spent each year in our country on our appearances. Let's ask a rather embarrassing question. Does that have anything to do with showing others we belong to Christ and he belongs to us? Suppose we shut down the industry for a year, except for certain basics like soap and water. Would this greatly hinder the cause of the Christian faith? Perhaps the chief argument would be that such a move would put numerous people out of work. Well, that becomes quite a dilemma, doesn't it? In complete seriousness, I wonder why it is essential for many Christians to do what they do in order to appear attractive. You may want to ask me what rock I crawled out from under, but hear me out. There is a requirement that we be sincerely holy people. In our depths, we know this is true and we are not bad people. Perhaps we have not yet gone far enough.

Our bodies are temples and that is awesomely spiritual. Each of us lives in a different body but we are all in temples. It is questionable if most Christians accept that and yet I do not want to be critical. My personal experience tells me quickly, and more directly than I like, there is much in my life — past and present — that needs to be washed by the blood of the Lamb of God. Those of us who have been given good health for many years can be too proud and ungrateful. Have you seriously thanked God today for health and financial resources? Always what we have is from God. Yes, what did you and I earn or create? Once in a while our singular greatness can blind us! If we are to be successfully retrieved, we are to remember we were bought with a price.

In the United States of America we are blessed with opportunities beyond the imaginations of millions living in other countries. Often they see our standard of living as something to acquire. In our inadequacy we tend to allow them to measure us in material success. How wrong this is! Perhaps this is where solid media emphasizing Christian unity and inter-religious dialogue come into play. Don't misunderstand me, some really good things are being done. More — much more — needs to be done. Christians flaunting their good fortune in terms of material success just isn't right! Getting things straight, really, is to trim the fat and live more healthy lives that exalt the Christ. Fractured moral lives that tend toward immorality then can be placed where they belong: the local trash heap. God is faithful to lead us to less meaning more for him.

3. Chastity may be unwelcome but it is the Christian's call.

Misuse of the body, especially in sexual activity, is one of the most pressing issues of our day and time. There are those who insist it ranks number one because it influences every area of society. Where can we begin with such a gargantuan problem? Good people who practice the Christian faith say they don't have the slightest idea! It is so complicated, and what is chastity anyway? Is it a simple refraining from actual intercourse between a man and a woman? May God the Father, Son, and Holy Spirit mercifully aid us as we attempt to work our way through this labyrinth of definitions. How can we teach our children and youth that sex is sacred?

Two becoming one flesh in a deeply religious sense is fodder for the late night comedians and comediennes. Shunning fornication would likely bring the biggest laugh! Saint Paul is deeply serious, as usual, and in tune with values that have consistently been a part of the Judeo-Christian tradition. I suspect many of us would be hard-pressed to come up with a person(s) who is prudish as we commonly understand it. Of course, that may not be all bad in view of the fact human nature after all is sinful and allowances for repentance and forgiveness are absolutely necessary. Surely we don't have to be caught between a rigid moral code that lacks compassion and a licentious lifestyle that preaches anything goes. We must pray daily for our young people to abstain from sexual activity until marriage becomes realizable.

In a Christian sense, how can the prospective bride and bridegroom prepare for the wedding vows, promising until death do they part? We might suggest for them to begin as new teenagers to promise to be chaste until they are married. Would the great bulk of those in our churches consider this a doable way of maturing? Those that I know would be serious and concerned but they would not go that far. Our Catholic friends can be of help here. They have a long-standing teaching of chastity and virginity. It has been there since the very early centuries and in a way is underlined by speaking of Jesus' mother as the blessed Virgin Mary. In addition, marriage is considered a sacrament. Yes, all of us can learn a great deal of practical idealism from them!

Then, there is this business of all situations being relative. This has been with us now officially for more than two generations. In reality I believe you can make a case for it beginning with Adam and Eve! Paul is not speaking of relativity in sexual matters as a way to live victoriously under the banner of Christ. Assuredly, he recognizes the curse of our first two parents and understands the tremendous harm that is done by sexual activity outside of the marriage vows. With all the relationships, divorces, and remarriages in our society how can we put Humpty Dumpty back together again? First, we must decide to practice total faithfulness in marriage with one wife or husband. Then, we must teach our children by precept and examples this way of life. Temptations are many and subtle today. In our weakness God's power is available.

79

4. Our bodies need our ongoing and loving attention.

It would be a mistake to spiritualize Paul's understanding of our bodies into making them ghostlike and non-biological in function. He is instructing us about what we can see and touch. Our arms, heads, hands, lungs, livers, feet, and all parts are his consideration. We are made in the image of God and therefore are to be stewards of what God, not ourselves, have created. To accept Christ as Savior and Lord does not mean we forsake or belittle our bodies for superior spiritual reasons! True, we eventually die and our bodies become dust but in the meantime we are to be good stewards. This means we neither abuse nor misuse what is entrusted to us.

The longer I live the more I am convinced there is an art to caring for our bodies. This art begins by our recognition of the gift coupled with the responsibility for it. Regardless of our sizes and shapes, beauty or lack of it, and physical prowess, it is ours and we are supposed to take care of it. That is not only a spiritual directive but common sense. Most of what is needed to apply this art can be learned, unless we run into major health problems or accidents. There is no need to make something difficult when, for the most part, it isn't. Money may or may not be needed. Physicians and other professionals may or may not be needed. God's gift is to be handled with tender loving care and at times that may mean strong medicines of discipline. Give thanks for our mortal bodies.

To be fruitful is to take good care of yourself. This is a reasonable expectation and has no bearing on a vain spirit, unless we make it so. Clergy too often try to go seven days and seven nights each week only to learn that is not the way we are made. We are guilty of attempts to please others that jeopardizes our health and in time it will show in our bodies, unless we make needed adjustments. We can feel good about ourselves — in the best and highest sense — provided we heed Paul's marvelous instruction. Every Christian is expected to produce fruit and the way we generally do this the best is by taking good care of ourselves. If we are excessively smoking and drinking alcohol, how can we be in top shape to do the Lord's work?

When our lives become fragments, especially the misuse of our bodies in a sexual way, look out! Case after case shows the apostle is on target. Someone rather elderly said to me that life is much more than sex and, of course, that is true. Yet, note the part it has played in our lives. What have we done about the devastating hurt that can potentially come from supposedly little missteps? Yes, Paul is right. We need to get it straight from the inspired rabbi. In our entirety, we are meant for the Lord. Anything short of that is not good enough. Ask God to save you from the misconception we can do his will and pay little attention to our bodies. Of course, the worst, unhealthy fiasco is to be caught in an adulterous relationship and to believe you can continue it and serve God. Likewise, prostitution is more than a lark. It is two becoming one flesh.

Summary And Conclusion
Saint Paul is the man of the hour in his instructive words to us. The world and especially those who claim Christ as Savior and Lord are to pay close attention. Living our lives in fragments is more than wrong; it is destructive to the brink of disaster. Our bodies, here and now, are created to be in full union with the Lord. Every part and portion is to belong to him. Stewardship is imperative. Sexual misdeeds, whatever form they take, must be labeled for what they are: a means to send our immortal souls to hell. Our bodies are not merely flesh and blood; they are temples of the Holy Spirit. Praises be to God for our precious bodies!

The sharpness and transparency of the text gives us reason to pause in silence and ponder its magnificent simplicity. In short, many of us will say these are difficult words out of step with our times but they bear a full gift of truth. The crux of the matter is at hand for those who profess the Father's Son. Will we believe wholeheartedly in the apostle's strong and firm advice or will we accommodate the pressures of living in a mostly secularized society? While many Christians must work in environments not at all conducive to such teaching being implemented, what shall we give in exchange for our immortal souls? Let us always allow for compassion and mercy. However, let us always be faithful to the revealed word of the living God. If we are now living our precious lives in morally destructive fragments, plead with God for help!

Being Single-minded

Introduction

The Second Coming of Christ was much in the thoughts of the ancient church. Saint Paul was no exception, as his letters often indicate. Time was growing short and soon the present form of this world would be passing away. The expectation must have been both thrilling and somewhat ominous for Christ's people.

There is a particularity about the events coming soon after our Lord's Ascension and the Day of Pentecost. A single-mindedness is virtually demanded. It all has to do with a single God/man they knew was the one in whom they found their salvation. He had given them more than hope. He had given them assurances of heaven with him.

In one sense, nothing has changed during those twenty centuries. We are to be centered on the one and only certain Savior of humankind, that little Jewish boy born of Mary. As he made his way as a lad and to maturity, including dying a terrible death and conquering the grave, anticipation filled the air. He was the Father's Son!

So, we are called to immerse ourselves completely in him, leaving no stone unturned. It is a radical invitation that begins and ends with him, and him alone. Perhaps we could use the cliché "the more things change, the more they are the same." Christ bids us to come both to die and arise with him.

Focus

We belong totally to Christ and no other.

Body

1. We are to believe in Christ for our salvation.

The radical and unequivocal nature of such a dogmatic stance has caused highly tensioned feelings in countless numbers. Yet, if we believe in the New Testament as the inspired word of God, both our choice and answer are clear. To live changed lives with the promise of heaven is our positive plight and all that entails. For those of us who have accepted Jesus Christ as the way, the truth, and the life we have, at least, an elementary understanding of the price we must pay. Also, by the grace of God, we have a built-in resource that refuses to be defeated. We don't always like what we are doing or refraining from doing but that is mostly irrelevant!

One's salvation is the most highly valued possession we have. It is who and what we are. To some extent, everyone has salvation or a set of beliefs and behavior patterns that manifest themselves. Even the cold and committed communist has this! Some follow and are absorbed by various ideologies but we must be very careful to stay the course with our Savior, who is Christ the Lord. Some say, almost derisively he/she finds identity only in his/her job. Well, I guess in a way that's we Christians! People and positions come and go in our lives but our true occupation or vocation remains the same. To live differently from this is to invite spiritual complications that only tend to muddle and postpone what (who) is intended for us.

The interreligious nature of today's world must be confronted and hopefully reconciled in ways helpful for all concerned. Arguments are seldom useful, especially if they are heated arguments before numbers of people. Our call is one to dialogue as peacefully as we can — in particular — among Jews and Muslims. Respect is always necessary. After all, aren't they also God's children? Yes, and do we presume to know all the ways God has and does deal with all of his dear children? Of real assistance along this line is a reading and pondering of Romans 9, 10, and 11. All three religions have Abraham for their father. Our call to radical living under the banner of Christ does not close the door to intelligent and dutiful dialogue.

Who has to have the greatest influence in our lives? Friends, this is a no-brainer! We are to be immersed in the healing waters of his love. It is a love that knows no bounds. It reasonably follows that such a style of living will rub off on others. In the Christian context, not to be fishers of men and women is a sad commentary and contradiction. To be sure, idealism is much at work here and we may try to be more than we are intended to be. Frankly, I don't think we should be overly worried about this. Remember, to pray that every day is successful in God's sight and not ours. This is a brilliant conditioner that allows us a kind of holy objectivity, which can immensely aid our spiritual growth. To live every day in his shadow is not to live in darkness but in light the world scoffs at and finds mostly meaningless. Christ beckons for us to be fully open to him.

2. All our bets are placed in Christ.

Casino gambling, as well as numerous other forms of gambling, seem to have become more and more popular in our nation. All of the reasons are well beyond me, but I do believe the one that comes quickly to the forefront is the chance for a winner to become independently wealthy and create an image of power in the recipient. Such a windfall brings immediate attention and both positive and negative recognition. It is a way of becoming somebody overnight and the realization that what was once out of reach financially, is no longer true. Christians take all we have and are; then we bet them on the belief Christ is the answer to our sins and incompleteness.

From the time we are small, some of us were taught not to put all of our eggs in one basket. Then, in a spiritual sense, that is exactly what we are inspired to do! Perhaps the thought occurs to us from time to time, that if we are wrong in our decision, we have lived a wasted life. It is a sobering thought. For the thinking person it makes perfectly good sense, even though it can be depressively destructive. To have lived and died in vain is perhaps the most horrendous thought a sane human being can have. It can send terrifying chills running up and down our backs. At its worst, urges to commit suicide come upon us. Paul would tell us confidently and firmly he hasn't changed his mind. All bets, not just some or most, are placed on the master, the man of Galilee. This is the way our lives are intended. There is no change on the horizon!

The gift we have and the grace provided to be encompassed by it is one that those with a mostly secular orientation to life will not understand. Some days I am not sure how much the dear Lord's disciples understood it! It is in our willing spirit and temperament of heart that we discover such magnificence to be worked out. It really isn't news but there is a genuine difference between Christ's people and the world. That does not mean we are to run away and hide for fear of contamination. However, it certainly does mean we have placed our bets on the Father's Son. We are risk takers, betting 100 percent on the authenticity of our salvation here and now and forever and ever. It is the right thing to do!

Are you satisfied with all of this? Would you rather it be some other way? Perhaps you would like to travel about the country or even the world, placing your bets in different casinos. Then, at least, you would have the chance of winning under various cir-cumstances. The saying, "winning some and losing some" may be a more shrewd approach to what you understand life to be. Don't bet on it! Saint Paul is lurking around with compassion but a firm hand, telling you in no uncertain terms to get with the revealed program. It is difficult to imagine him humorous, except possibly to prove the point he lived and died by. If you want to squander some extra cash with a cult or new age guru, this could be quite an eye-opener and lead to betting everything on Christ. It could also put you on a demonic roller coaster that eventually runs with an outrageous and fatal ending.

3. Our destiny is tied to Christ.

We are a peculiar people. One extraordinary man was born into history who we say is God in the flesh. We worship him and call him several names but, in particular, Savior and Lord. Our revelation in the New Testament indicates without reservation he was with the Father from the beginning. Securely linked to this Son, we are locked into a unique relationship for all time and even when time is dissolved as a principle found in creation. Wow! Isn't that mind-boggling? Indeed, we are a peculiar people. This is so much true we, at times, have laborious moments attempting to communicate with others the supposedly simple story of Jesus. It is hard to come up with all the superlatives!

It is as though we are owned by him and have become his slaves. Well, we were bought with a price and that was his precious and holy blood. To attempt to tell of our destiny separate and apart from this Jewish fellow, is most difficult — if not impossible. What we have to tell the world in joy and humility is the unparalleled satisfaction we have. If we go all the way with him, we have a peace that passes all understanding. That does not mean we are free from various kinds of pain or even, at times, serious doubts. It is more than a change of pace. It is joy unspeakable that remains calm in the face of the lovely becoming decidedly unlovely. Yes, it is likened to the man who searched the world over and found the pearl of great price, discarding gladly all the others.

Whenever the end comes, either with the Second Coming or our deaths, we are hopeful in ways foreign to those who do not have this Savior and Lord. Well, are we claiming too much? Is Paul pointing us in a direction that is never realized? Are we so peculiar we have our heads in the sand and could possibly be having hallucinations? My answer to this not uncommon inquiry is, "But, my dear friends, have you tried it?" As that answer is being given we must never assume power in our own strength. As Paul discovered, God's grace is sufficient because his power is made perfect in weakness. This is an imperative we must learn, hopefully early! We were bought with the supreme price of the Father's Son.

When the end for us comes in this life, are we prepared to have a glimpse of our funeral service and place of burial? Are the ushers and pallbearers the ones we have chosen? Will good and accurate things be said about us? Will our family and friends be present to bid us farewell? It is only human nature to ask such questions but aren't they all secondary? Some of us, more than anything else, want to hear our family and friends assuredly say he/she was a genuinely good person whose destiny was unquestionably tied to the ever-living Christ. The here and now meets eternity. Our witness is given and preserved because of his love for us and our response of giving ourselves unconditionally. Any artist would be hard-pressed to show this on a canvas or writer in a book. On our knees in silence or with heads high, shouting his praises, we are going to our real home.

4. We are to stay focused and live accordingly.

Anyone in the workaday world knows the importance of staying focused. Perhaps this has always been true but in the current era the demands are such that most would never hold a job for any length of time unfocused. The computer has much to do with this, and certainly the ever-increasing sophistication with intricate maneuvering is another. Our grandparents and even parents — depending on our age — would likely find few ways even to begin to comprehend what's going on in the workforce today. That is not in any way to cast aspersions. Since we were not at our peaks in their day, maybe we should note that their focusing may have been far more physically demanding.

The single-minded follower of Christ is different from the world at large. In the first place, we shut out the clamor of those who would rob us of our spiritually esteemed place. We do not necessarily devalue the world and its trimmings. After all, we certainly need it to survive! Our secret is in not allowing hurtful forces to take over our time, energy, and talents. In short, we stay focused on Christ and live accordingly. In the second place we never forget from whom our help comes. We do not save ourselves and we are not smart enough to provide the guidance essential for victorious living. We admit leaning on the everlasting arms is more than words set to music. A drummer different from that orchestrated by the world is continually at work. We love the angels singing.

The enemy of our souls has countless tools at his disposal. They come in shades and sizes we may or may not recognize. As some revivalists of yesteryear used to say, "Even the devil quotes scripture." To maintain there is no such evil force is to be blinded to the spiritual reality of our great leaders who paved the way for us. It seems the most persuasive person can be on the payroll of the one who tempted our Lord in the wilderness. You and I can readily recognize all of this at work, only to learn we are also at the brink of being duped! Note how easily we are led astray simply by getting us to focus in directions where Christ is not present.

Our lives tell stories. Others listen to them. Some watch them. We are on display! The Christian witness calls attention to itself in ways intended to be powerfully positive. We are being graded. That doesn't mean the teachers always know what they are talking about. It does mean they are either trying to tear down what they experience or desire what we have. We must not fail or if we do, quickly repent with forgiveness and continue our spiritual journey. So much is intended for all of us! The table is filled to overflowing with goodies. Praise God from whom all blessings flow. Friends, stay focused and live accordingly under the banner of Jesus Christ. While God is all-powerful, he still uses our hands, feet, minds, and hearts to carry the gospel of his Son. To whom do we belong? There is only one correct answer: Jesus Christ. All others are secondary.

Summary And Conclusion

Spiritually speaking, a scatter-brained person is in serious trouble! We cannot live our precious lives this way and that way, expecting to have the assurance of salvation. To wander across the fields of this and that provides only an unrest that may last a lifetime. Let the externals come and go. Let them be good times and bad times. Let friends come and go. Just be sure your interior life is in peaceful acceptance of Christ. Have we not heard? Jesus is primarily interested in our hearts. He wants to reside there permanently and do for us what we can never do for ourselves. Yes, we — at our very best — belong totally to Christ and no other. He provides a safety net for all of humanity. He continues to knock on the doors of those who have spurned his love, some for a lifetime.

The popularity of Second Coming publications is, at times, unbelievable. The hungry public in large numbers never seem to get their fill, and lots of money is made. Our call is not to be caught up in something we really have never known much about. In fact, our Lord tells us only the Father knows the day or night. Our major mode of living always has directly to do with the man born in a manger. If he returns right now, fine. If he returns, centuries from now, fine. We are to stay focused on to whom we belong. Not only that but rid ourselves of any competitor. Jesus will not tolerate others before him. In a way it is the restoration of one of the Ten Commandments. Be steadfast and of good cheer. Hold fast to that you know is satisfaction *par excellence!*

Looking Out For Others

Introduction
Being able to synthesize in such a way that harmony can be
the outcome is among the many things the Apostle Paul does well.
The often-pesky church at Corinth desperately needed such a skill,
written and practiced in charity. To follow his inspired advice comes
as a gift to all of us, 2,000 years ago or today.

The individualistic Christianity, largely the work of Protestants,
has been and is both a bane and balm, for us. To do our own thing
is commendable and perhaps essential but it can prove utterly destructive to those who cannot comprehend the diversity found in
our faith. Think what great problems we have solved and yet left
unsolved!

We are to look out for others, especially if we are more mature
in the faith. However, this can be an open door to tragedy, unless
we remember to keep a close eye on our imperfect lives. But Paul
makes his point about as perfectly as it can be made. We walk
away from it and discover Satan is staring us in the face.

Charity for one another is the way great and powerful congregations are built. It is also the way we as individuals become more
than private disciples, ministering mostly to ourselves. The Pauline
teaching does not disappoint unless we pay little real attention to
it.

Focus
We are called spiritually to form others, as well as ourselves.

Body

1. Weak believers are always among us.

Even as we speak about the weakness of others, we are reminded of how weak we were initially in practicing the Christian faith. It seems to me we should be in a penitent mood every time we seek gently to correct others. They are where we were. But let's not be too quick to celebrate a permanent level of maturity. My experience is that even the saints from time to time fall from lofty and respected heights. The history of the church provides excellent examples. However, we do know those who went through such episodes became stronger. Even though they wept bitterly, as did Saint Peter, the powerful pain of it all enabled them not only to return to their former level but above it.

It is so important to practice what we preach before our weaker brothers and sisters. When can we ever say to them "don't do as I do, but do as I say"? The folly of lip service to the religion Christ gave to us is probably the most disastrous event in our lives in the long run. While this may sound harsh, pastors can be the most outlandishly guilty of all! We can preach tithing but do we tithe? We can preach praying constantly but do we do so? We can preach about daily study and pondering of the Holy Scriptures but do we practice this, except for Sunday preaching? We can preach about solid and ongoing relationships with other denominations but are we available to the pastor down the street?

For those content in their Christian living, it can be quite a jolt to learn there is a basic responsibility for others. We all know these lovely people, who are often prime movers or — at least — faithful to what they have been willing to accept. The proud and highly respected pastor or layperson may enjoy the attention and recognition so much he/she is unable to detect spiritual blindness. Some of us not only know such people but we have been there, haven't we? Experience teaches me there is a creative discontent in our lives that is not always welcome. We learn things we would just as soon not learn! Of course, we can all say we care for others but do we do so as the Holy Spirit has guided us?

There is what I call a grumbling syndrome among God's people. That can be at any level of the church or in any individual's life.

Hopefully, this is a means for the spiritually strong to enable the weak to become more like the crucified and resurrected Lord. Sometimes, even the most devoted soul perceives negatives and perhaps actual defeat, only to learn joyously we have passed through a phase lifting all of us higher. These are times of thanksgiving for what the Holy Spirit has been able to accomplish. Be alert to them because they certainly do happen! To grumble is not a sin in my opinion, unless it becomes an unquenchable thirst that is never satisfied. Sometimes those who are weak need something new and different in their lives virtually on a daily basis. Perhaps the news media has aided and abetted this!

2. Liberty in thought and action is intended to benefit others.

Isn't this what the United States of America is about? In our idealism — since the beginning — we have sought to make this a guiding principle. Sure, we attempted to improve ourselves individually but in doing so we likewise — at least at an idealistic level — wanted the same opportunities for others. We have always been a melting pot and continue to be. While at first this may not seem to have a direct bearing on Paul's teaching; it shows the influence of a definite belief in human rights. Truly, our nation has been a beacon to millions! Our Puritan fathers and mothers may not have understood this at first but there were forces that made them bend.

Isn't it a glorious sight to watch others grow in the faith? That's especially true if we have been a part of it. Oh, I don't mean we can document it! Mostly, our contributions don't come about that way. How fortunate we are because that means we cannot brag about it! Some Christian's are truly a work of art, as they go about being formed in the likeness of Christ. Their independence and sometimes brashness eventually becomes a gift for the wider body of believers. As experimentation comes and goes, the Holy Spirit synchronizes, harmonizes, and sometimes formalizes. Precious and essential spiritual formation glows for all to see, that is, those who are attentive. "Life, liberty, and the pursuit of happiness" are not necessarily secular terms.

The greats of our faith are those who have often reached out, creating high levels of frustration and more. They have also in some cases been those who have pulled back in order to bring others along that were weak in the faith. Perhaps the most notable personage is Pope John XXIII, who flung open the windows of the Catholic church but refused to abandon the revelation of the faith, as he understood it. While he has his critics, the Catholic church has never been the same and yet it is still the same! The widening and broadening of his pontificate made the Catholic church far more accessible to others, especially inquirers. Such beacons never made the mistake of Napoleon Bonaparte, who invaded Russia and moved too far from his supply lines!

The flow of religious and moral ideas across all lines is a major achievement for our time. To be sure, problems — some of them enormous — have been created. Yet, with the mind of Christ, rooted and grounded in the faith, we are able to discriminate among the uplifting and hurtful. In the cauldron of multicultural existence there is that momentous opportunity to grow more fully, totally, and completely into the likeness of Jesus Christ. Denominational lines often have come tumbling down. When they didn't, sometimes new forms for ministry were given birth. Shades of the Wesleys and the Church of England! So, let us give thanks for the wonders of our day and time, despite the very real potential for unimaginable holocausts. May the will of the Father be done!

3. We are to make a contribution to every life we touch.

Well, that sounds like a big order, doesn't it? There is a profound truth here that may not dawn on us until we are well along in years. Is it too much to expect? Definitely not, that is, if we seriously believe that all things are possible with God. As the Holy Spirit works through us, for us, and among us, each and every precious human being we touch can be benefited. In terms of prayerful extension many others can also be influenced for the good. To make a difference for good in another person's life is actually a reasonable expectation. To be flexible enough to enable others to see the Christ more completely is ministry, pure and simple.

Many of us — if not all — have wondered upon occasion about our positive presence. Not being able to sense growth in others tends to be a common experience. However, it is certainly true that when the most severe darkness comes, we are soon to witness the sun coming up. Perhaps for you that is not always the case, but frankly it has been true over and over again for me. Spiritual formation generally is not an easy matter. To move ahead of others and then be called to look back to their state and pick them up is not something many of us enjoy. After all, in our competitive world isn't it the American way to keep stretching ourselves and solidifying our positions? In spiritual dynamics we know this is not the way to go. The weak are to be treated with dignity and respect. God expects that of us!

Our prayers should be focused upon this very concept. We are to aid in forming others and not run away to some safe corner to sit in a rocking chair. Prayer remains the most powerful force in benefiting others. Of course, we are to keep in mind this may be a prelude to actual and open change. In others we set the table and before you know it, luscious food and drink appear to enhance our friends who are on the same pilgrimage. Being only a novice in spirituality, I do suspect the most telling battles of this world are fought in the prayers of righteous people. The prayers of the American people, as well as many others, have had to be colossal in their impact on history.

Some winsome people in my churches have worshiped most Sundays in the year and given generously of their money. As a pastor, when you ask about their prayer lives you hit a thud. It simply hasn't been developed! To participate in public worship and give our money are commendable. There is one more thing more commendable: prayer. Why? Because this is catching the ear of God and provides little or no statistical success. The success comes in relationship with the Father, Son, and Holy Spirit. Many have marveled at the prayers given by grandparents, parents, brothers/sisters, and others. While we have no overt proof in a scientific sense, how many of us were formed spiritually by them? Their contribution is more than we can repay, except in the obvious. We, too, can pray for those coming after us. They may or may not be relatives. Whoever they are, they need our prayers today and tomorrow.

4. Our lives are never lived in a vacuum.

Some appear to believe there is a space completely empty, except for them. Christianity is a relational faith. From the outset it assumed we would be in touch with others — laughing, crying, or celebrating. Our Lord's visits to secret places for prayer never became permanent. It must likewise be true for us. To build fences and walls around ourselves not only excludes others, but we are also excluded and do not receive the benefits intended. It is not always easy to let other people into our lives and there may be good reasons. Perhaps you have let a person into your life and been used. Perhaps you have confided in someone, only to learn the confidence was broken.

We have records of hermits who lived isolated lives and rarely saw anyone. This can be something quite different! There are those who take vows and spend years in seclusion on behalf of the kingdom of God. It is an extraordinary person who can do this. For you and me, plus virtually everyone we know, such an experience and way of life is foreign. Let us not magnify these isolated ways of living and call them the epitome of practical spirituality. Of course, we must not vilify such men and women that truly and wholesomely live a life of poverty, chastity, and obedience. For the average Mr. Church (man or woman) we are aware of our spiritual vocation to aid in spiritually forming others. As we benefit others, we benefit ourselves. All disciples committed to the Christ have known this at some level.

Christ also died for weak believers! Just because we may have more maturity, does not mean the crucifixion was more for us and somehow we are favored in the Father's eyes. Those words at first may hit you as strange and even humorous but take a moment or longer to test your depths. By our works and apparent successful living, are we better off spiritually than others? Am I seriously my brother's (sister's) keeper? It is an old question posed well before the Christian era. Are congregations guilty of separating into the haves and the have-nots? Had the pastor best be working with the haves in order to save time and cut down on his/her frustrations? In our souls there are times for whatever reasons we know this happens. Pastors, for the most part, learn early that the institution must be maintained at the corner of 10th and Elm!

God's patience saves the day for most of us, sometimes quoting our passage from Saint Paul back to us. There is this responsibility to look out for others and it doesn't go away. Those who get on our cracked nerves also belong to the family. They may be weak and — in our minds — a waste of time but that does not make them less a part of the family. Are they spiritually underprivileged because they just don't have the smarts? That is a terribly arrogant question and yet it must be asked. We cannot go our merry way and extricate ourselves from that which is difficult, trying our patience to the limits. We are all sinners saved by the grace of God. In our precious salvation the Father is merciful to both the weak and strong.

Summary And Conclusion

Knowledge can, in the Pauline sense, be a burden to us and produce an arrogance that alienates our brothers and sisters. We are reminded that love builds up and, sooner or later, everyone benefits. This is frequently not the way the world views people and things. The more degrees and professional experience we have, the more spiritually fruitful we are. Who are we trying to mislead? Love is what carries the day in good times and bad times. There are times Ph.D.s must learn from those who have never been to college or perhaps not even graduated from high school. Of course, we must not discount the possibility of academia and piety being an integral part of the same person. To tout ones ignorance and immaturity in childish ways is not what Saint Paul had in mind!

Our friend, Paul, is a brilliant teacher. He explains and challenges by turns. To get in a full-fledged argument with him must have been a powerfully painful experience! He strikes at the heart of the problem frequently present in our faith in the past and present. We can hear him saying love is patient and kind. It is also not jealous or boastful. You and I may need to test the waters of our real maturity again. We may need to have the cobwebs cleared from our hearts, so we can once again feel and understand we are to look out for others. This is not optional! Our trespasses are forgiven as we forgive others their trespasses. Regardless of your leadership role in the life of the church, covenant with the Father to be the person Christ desires you to be, with whomever you find yourself.

A Man For All Seasons

Introduction

The enigma of human relationships and how that relates to the living God is all about us. It always has been and likely will be. This is precisely what Saint Paul lifts up before us. We would like for all of this to be greatly simplified but it never is and so we continue to seek to live the Christian life as best we know how.

The history of the church is saturated with just what the apostle puts before us. In a way we are caught between two worlds and we have no choice. We live as well we can and hope for heaven. Sometimes our difficulties emerge because we fail to realize God is the God of both of them. The world may be corrupt and fallen but he has not abdicated his throne!

Our freedom, like Paul's, is one of countless dimensions and allows us to relate to precious people in ways we can hardly imagine. This is a privilege and a powerful dynamic, I dare say, many do not understand in the slightest degree. While the gospel is not for boasting, it is for proclamation and we must not fail to do so!

In a sense he is God's "secret weapon" in that he is able to stand with an unfulfilled Judaism and a promising religion evolving from it called Christianity. Perhaps no one in the ancient church was as well qualified and equipped. History bears this out in a remarkable fashion.

Focus

We are to be resilient for the sake of Christ.

99

Body

1. There are good politics and bad politics.

Politics — in the general sense — is inescapable in this life. To relate to other human beings, sooner or later, invariably becomes political. Every pastor of a local church, for example, is a politician! Does that cast doubt on the integrity of his/her leadership? I certainly hope not. As pastor and people live and work together, we know that management of time, talents, and money must take place. To think otherwise is unrealistic. To act otherwise is most likely to court disaster. Political science is an esteemed field of study, but the practical side of it takes it not only out of academia but out of the basic understanding of those connected to governmental processes.

To cast off concerns and issues as just being politics is to assume a negative aspect that is often not there. For example, every church and/or denomination has a polity. Simply stated, how else do we expect to function in this imperfect world? We can accuse others of playing politics, including Paul, but does that mean we are free and clear in our own less-than-ideal bailiwicks? This state of affairs has always been with us, regardless if we operated by episcopal, congregational, or presbyterial models. To get things done, even in the life of the churches, we frequently have to play politics in the highest and best sense of the term. This can be construed as being negative and below what Christ expects. However, do we really want to do his bidding?

Resiliency is not an option in our walk with others, yes, even in our churches. Survival in this sometimes obviously sinful world means to get the best answer or decision by the grace of God. Must we feel guilty because of this? Must we hang our heads in shame because we have failed to live up to the ideal? Frankly, and without reservation, I do not think so! Good politics means above all — sincerely calling upon the Father for guidance and letting the chips fall where they fall. We cannot flounder in a briar patch just because we refuse to make of it the best it can be under the circumstances. Of course, all veteran pastors and lay people deep down know this, often with a certain painful joy.

As our man for all seasons weaves his way through the necessary means of winning others, we experience a genius at work. All is done for the sake of the gospel and winning others to the cause of Christ. Perhaps it is seen as a method for him and not for us. Let us not be naive! The political machinations of this world are with us and that means in the honest to goodness lives of the people called Christians. But politics can be good, which can mean sacrificing our brilliance for the betterment of all involved. But, dear friends, never be a secularized politician, which is always self-seeking and devoid of the undergirding of prayer. Always look out for the spiritual interests of others and always bathe your means and ends in humble and sincere prayer. Otherwise, we could become an anathema!

2. We are called to be adjustable in the best sense of the word.

At first, our point may sound like we must be amenable to being tossed to-and-fro by others. Nothing could be further from the truth! For in the best sense none of us has all of the answers to anything or anyone. Think about all of the answers we don't even have about ourselves. In the United Methodist system of appointments — some would add disappointments — adjustments continually have to be made. The moving of one pastor generally means, at least, two others are moving as well. This involves negotiation with large amounts of patience by all concerned. My experience is that district superintendents really do attempt to make good appointments.

Anyone, lay or clergy, unable to adjust to new pastors and people are in serious trouble. This is true, regardless of the polity. Our needs sometimes simply have to go unmet for awhile. But this should never discourage us. Why? Because from every situation into which we are put, we can learn something valuable. That one truth is frequently the key to maturing in the faith for all of us. So, give thanks and be adjustable under the working of the Holy Spirit that blows wherever it chooses. What we are and become is for the sake of Christ and his one, holy, catholic, and apostolic church. Our walk with the Lord is sooner or later a learning experience. Stretching out to others and making the necessary adjustments should be — in time — a highly positive experience. Our spiritual muscles are always in need of growth!

One direction is not being promoted or recommended and that is what is popularly known as "going with the flow." There are times that we must stand our ground. This is especially true as we come into contact with those who are not interested in the church or may even be an enemy. If we are going with the flow, we must be as certain as possible such movement has the blessing of God and is being directed by the Holy Spirit. Disciples of Christ are exactly that. They have no other to worship and follow. The enemy, the devil, also has ways of putting us in places and positions that require adjustments fraught with serious — perhaps damning — consequences. Remember your childlikeness before the Father!

Conforming in our lives is both obvious and subtle. This is why changes in the life of congregations are to be made above board. For the pastor to slip one over on someone is no cause for jubilation. In fact, it may be the cause of much aggravation. To arrange or rearrange something for the good of the whole church, where adjustments are necessitated, calls for open discussion and a generous spirit. You may very well say such an approach is merely common sense and, yes, we do things that way. Don't be too sure! When we are in a hurry to meet a goal, we may cut some corners. Those empowered with responsibility and authority, lay and clergy, are to be keenly sensitive. This is not to imply everyone needs to know the number of paper clips in the secretary's desk on a given day in order to trust her.

3. To stretch in different directions in the Holy Spirit benefits all.

I am a great believer in stretching with the Holy Spirit as presence and guidance. That is not said in a way to become an annoyance or to become aggressive. It is to suggest we move forward in the faith by moving into new experiences. The progressive people tend to be continually exploring and seeking new opportunities for doing good. Those who remain stagnant seem always to be in the same places, unwilling to stretch into areas of promise. The attitude is much like the farmer, who was offered a new parcel of land. He was firm in saying, "I know what is here but I don't know what is over there." He said that in the face of the fact the parcel was adjacent to his!

Stretching assumes resiliency and that may very well be why some are so hesitant and reluctant. But if we are to imitate Paul, we, too, must become men and women of all seasons for the benefit of others. It can become a dull ordeal to live in a place that has twelve months of spring or summer or winter or fall. In Indiana, we never have to face that problem because we have, at least, four seasons and once in a while it seems like a dozen or more! Likewise, our churches and constituencies can be more or less suffocated by those who cannot seem to move from point A to B. If both pastor and lay leadership fall into this category, of what use are they to bringing the gospel to those pleading for an open spirit?

Try to put yourself in the place of Paul and all that was facing him. He was surrounded by powers who were disinterested in his message and — in some instances — threatened by it. Yet, it was his responsibility to be among them stretching here and there to present the gospel of his blessed Lord. He is even willing to become weak in order that he might win them. Except before the Lord, it must have been quite a task for him to become weak for the purpose of trying to win others. As some of his writings indicate, he was surrounded on every side by those who wanted to compromise or destroy his message. There were some who even sought to obliterate the message of Christ by killing all who faithfully followed him, and we hold back because its either too hot or too cold outside!

The many-sided Christian is the one in today's world who is most effective. That does not mean we compromise or water down our gift from the Lord. While our anchor must be safe and secure, that does not preclude moving in waters — deep or shallow — to influence others for Christ and the church. There are those who would view this as a fragmented and therefore unacceptable approach to presenting the gospel. Paul did not give up the gospel he was trying to promote! We don't need to do that, either. Ideally, we are strong enough in the faith, as we move about, to provide a certain spiritual aroma that causes others to want what we have.

The more we can relate to them in their patterns of living, the more apt we are to be successful in their conversion.

4. Rigidity is sometimes a means to stunt the spiritual growth of others.

Old First Church sat on the corner of High and Elm for so many years — rigidly, as the community viewed it — that it had to be torn down before it fell down! It didn't have to be that way. New life seemed to come and go but it could never stay long enough to make the essential changes. So, those longing to have more of the Lord's blessings mostly passed through. It was as though the Holy Spirit kept on grieving until finally it refuses to grieve any longer. It was sad and depressing, but did God take care of those who wanted to grow? Indeed, he did! They went elsewhere and found those who were open to change that Christ might be more fully glorified.

Are conservatives more rigid than liberals? That is not a simple question and there is no simple answer. We live in a world, the churches included, where name-calling is common place and frozen thought is typical. Both sides have their agendas. Some are liberals along certain lines and conservative along others. Liberals often picture conservatives as those "religious right" people who are so closed-minded that they have no clear view of what's happening in the world. Conservatives tend to measure liberals by their wayward morality and failure to interpret the constitution in a proper manner. Entire books have been written on this topic. The definition of terms and spins put on key words and ideas are there to see for the keen observer.

Is contemporary worship in its many forms rigid? A cry may be going up, of course, that has to be answered in the negative. In fact, contemporary worship is to avoid rigidity in worship. I must confess to those proponents that is not automatically the case. I am reminded, years ago, of the church we attended when I was a child, which prided itself on never using printed orders of service because they didn't want to get in the way of the Holy Spirit. Leaders mentioned with frequency how those formal churches shut out God by their insistence on following a printed order. Years later, in retrospect, I recalled how in our little church everything moved orderly and there was little deviation but, of course, we had no bulletins. Any form of worship can become rigid and do the very thing it says it doesn't!

All in all, we are dependent both corporately and individually on being obedient to the Holy Spirit. This was Saint Paul's weapon. In whatever state he found himself he could be content because his resilient way of life in the Spirit was continually conquering evil that abounded. All is done for the sake of Christ. Can we do as well? Probably not but we can try in the strength that is promised and given to us. We are guilty of underestimating the power of our salvation and thereby stunt the growth of others. We sheepishly say — even emphasize — we can't do this or that. Our rigidity is held like some prize that requires constant vigil! In the meantime, events and happenings march on. Some people enter this world and others leave. Someone has need of your assistance.

Summary And Conclusion

The obligation of the apostle to proclaim the gospel is so deeply rooted he senses God will not hold him guiltless for refusing this call. His freedom and slave status are a paradox. In a way, it defies words to delineate it. Yet, towering in our New Testament is this remarkably unique man, who provides a witness for Christ and his church that never goes away. Perhaps our faith shall never again see such a positively resilient person going about doing the work of the Lord. His strength and spirit provide a model for us. We may discover ourselves far from this in practice. Nevertheless, the model is there and beckons us to come and learn from one of the geniuses of the faith.

Can we be too idealistic? Does the text suggest veering away from the purity of the gospel and making provision for an odious compromise? Of course, the answers must be yours. Humbly, I admit there may not be any crystal-clear answers. That only gently reminds me we are invariably living and ministering in an environment that contains mystery. A strictly rational approach to our salvation has always been filled with limitations. We have always, at one time or another, needed to take a leap of faith. So, dearest

Paul, we thank you for your insights that enable us to have hope in the conversion of a world, sinful and in desperate need of Christ. We also thank you for the hope that is engendered and gives us a look — imperfect and cloudy that it be — of our real home in heaven. We promise to work on in our little ways for now.

Plea For Discipline

Introduction

In a way, Christians are all in the Olympics! We are running the race that determines our eternal abode. We run to win and the prize is the most valuable we will ever seek. No money or property will purchase it. Only self-control under the banner of Christ grants a chance for winning.

The apostle is very clear and speaks to all who would enter the race that leads to everlasting life with the Father, Son, and Holy Spirit. It is an old/new teaching to whom all Christians for twenty centuries can relate. It is couched in terms both familiar and relevant.

For you and me, now early in the twenty-first century, it keeps us in touch with sublime revelation that remains at once practical and dependent on faith. As one ponders the brevity of one's life, the truth shines in all its splendor. This brief period of living on planet earth is but a dressing room for the main event.

God's grace allows and enables us to have this opportunity above all others to win the prize. The competition comes mostly from the evil one who does not want us to succeed and will do what's necessary to see that we don't. The track has numerous land mines and other devices, some very clever, either to make us fall and never get up or to quit the race altogether.

Focus

Self-control is imperative for authenticity.

Body

1. Freedom and self-discipline are not contradictory.

Many of us have a problem in keeping the two in harmony. On the surface, they certainly appear to be in contradiction, but we have as our guide Saint Paul who loved his freedom and yet preached and apparently practiced a rigid self-control. He shows us the way and builds his case convincingly. The wise men of the day might have a problem with living as he requires. Perhaps that is why he points out in different passages of his writings the need to rise above mere human wisdom. Christ leads us to higher heights and that is for the best and highest good: eternal life with the master.

I dare say free spirits are seldom seen as disciplined folks! They often are the most morally careless people on the face of this earth, delighting in shocking those about them. When you study the apostle's corpus of writings, you discover the two — freedom and discipline — existing side by side in creative tension. His understanding provides us with truth that transcends mere rules and regulations. It also gives us Christ's spirit which maintains all things are possible with God in the winds and sometimes hailstorms of the Holy Spirit. To debate this matter endlessly, much like predestination and free will, is fruitless and leads most likely to where we were never intended to go. Aren't we privileged to have a Savior and Lord who will victoriously see us through?

For us to become weak in order to be strong is cause for consternation and perhaps humiliation among some of us. Our disciplines will only take us just so far in our walk with the Lord, but they are essential. To admit to the need of self-control is a step all of us must take. To acknowledge the mystery of our freedom in this ongoing environment provides a way for peace that can pass the best of human understanding. Experience shows us that even the most dramatic of instantaneous conversions will cool off and lose their effectiveness, unless discipline is implemented. Our relationship with God is always a covenental one that is perhaps best described as a divine/human contract. God forbid that we ever view this as equals negotiating!

Our call is to faithfulness. People must be able to see authenticity in it, not only on Sunday mornings but at all times we are being observed. Every day of our lives we are being watched by others and being graded on whether or not we are *bona fide*. Generally, Christians live out our lives in fish bowls! To slip can be costly, even though in our hearts we are not wrongly motivated and before God have not sinned. But human nature, being what it is, does not allow us the luxury of letting our disciplines become so loosened others are given reason to say negative things about us and our faith. From that viewpoint, ours is seldom an easy life and the sooner we learn the devil is for real, the better off we are. We can never please everyone and that — lest we forget — is not our purpose.

2. Aimless wandering can be the loss of precious time.

The apostle would have us to understand we must be fixed on Christ and his requirements. There is a certain time consciousness built into his lesson for us. Our days and nights have a timekeeper. We call him the Father of us all. The cliché that we have just so much time may be something boring but it is good and important that we be reminded. Our waste of it is more than impractical, but if it persists, sinful, jeopardizing our eternal souls. Not only must we settle in on that which is absolutely basic to our well-being, we must do so with genuineness. There is to be much more than New Year's Eve's resolutions that diminish and die!

Remember a significant part of the word to us is that after we have proclaimed the gospel, we should not be disqualified. It is a sobering thought and indirectly pleads with us to make spiritually good use of our time. Wandering about, after telling others about the good news, can cause pastors painful grief. To tell your people about the Savior and then allow yourself to become an unsettled wayfarer is to invite an infectious attitude of loose living. Regardless of likes or dislikes, our parishioners do count on us to show them the way. Our most persistent critics sometimes will look to us in a pleading fashion to help them. Yes, the ordained pastor is in a special place before God and his/her people to be an example of right living and that means authentic self-discipline.

The plea for discipline is done in a framework most any person can understand. A race has time limitations. Measurements and judgments are made. The longer we delay running the race, the less time we have to compete. Procrastination, for whatever reason, lessens our chances of winning. How can you win, unless you enter the race? In the athletic world, professional or amateur, the facts are at hand. If you want to be a good runner, boxer, baseball player, or member of any other sports team, you can't wait until you are forty years old! Precious time has gone and it is gone forever in this life. Honest people, as they begin to get old, will occasionally share with us they have missed many opportunities. One blatant fact is time has not been treated with stewardship.

Enslaving our bodies may sound as though we are wrestling with sexual temptation. That may very well be but it also refers to all aspects of our lives that must be under discipline for the cause of Christ. Punishing our bodies for the cause of him who is the way, the truth, and the life is a noble effort. It is not *sadomasochism!* In reading the lives of the saints we discover fairly quickly this was a concern in their midst. What some of them underwent to be more completely servants of their Lord is a challenge to us. They understood their bodies were temples and to be treated with care and honor. Such treatment in their minds and hearts involved developing and maintaining authentic disciplines. This was accomplished not solely for their benefit but for the world to which they were mandated to minister.

3. Spiritual formation requires a disciplined heart and mind.

The two working together harmoniously gives us a willing spirit that seeks, above all, to do spiritual formation. Now, we are onto what makes glowing Christians, whose lives remind us of a well-oiled spiritual machine casting beneficial sunshine to others. Perhaps nothing provides greater salesmanship for the gospel of Jesus Christ. A miracle is at work that inspires other miracles in the lives of those needy human beings searching for something (someone) for which to live and die. It is a beautiful sight to behold, much like a lovely array of flowers that are perfectly blended with a fragrance which is captivating. Does this actually happen? Some of us can attest to it!

We are to remind ourselves, daily if need be, that our chief function and goal is to be an instrument in forming others after the likeness of him who died for us and arose again. This is accomplished only by disciplined living under the guidance of the Holy Spirit. Authenticity is at the core and is not to be negotiated away. This is no place for manipulation and intimidation. Falsification is an abomination. We are expected to hold up under verification every day of our lives. Praise God from whom all blessings flow! We have been given much and much is expected of us. While failure may have to be tolerated, it is never acceptable. Praise him all creatures here below!

Some of us know what it means for the heart and mind to be working in different directions. Even Saint Paul knew the experience of doing the very thing he hated because his mind was not up to the task of providing discipline. Spiritual heartbreak can be the result and more than oneself may be injured. Heartaches are born in such a milieu. At their worst, heart attacks wreak havoc on others, especially God's people. In the clergy we witness this as some fall morally, usually in succumbing to sexual misdeeds or handling money in suspicious ways. The heart is good but the mind is tested in attacking temptation and fails. Fantasies are allowed to grow, even encouraged, and Satan has his way. Clergy always are in need of our prayers.

Our Lord, as he neared the time of his crucifixion, gives us a splendid example of perfect submission to the will of the Father. The struggle has been there for all of us to read for centuries. His human will was tempted to weaken and find a way out. It was strong enough to do what the Father required. Who among us can even imagine the self-control necessary? Furthermore, who can even begin to imagine what would have transpired had his discipline failed. Would he have fled to another country? Would he have compromised with the Jewish and Roman authorities, so his life would have been spared? We can develop more scenarios. His discipline gloriously provided for the sacrifice for our sins and the salvation of humankind. In a matter of hours, saying, "Yes," to

God the Father and, "No," to his human nature changed the world forever and ever.

4. Disqualification for God's kingdom is always a tragedy.

Our text concludes with the realism of which Paul was typically capable. What a shame to go about telling others about the good news and its requirements, only to become disqualified yourself! Christ emphasizes not to judge others and God will not judge us. Yet, over a period of years and in different parishes, it indeed seems to happen. Once in a while, there is a shocker with a pillar of the church coming unglued and crashing down in most every way. We never want to dwell on these negative happenings but let's admit the possibility is continually present.

Letting down our guard in a spiritual sense lays the groundwork for problems, big and small. Evil forces will slip under our radar and eat away at the finest teaching we know. Now and then Christians decide to go on a questionable lark. What is anticipated as being fun, relaxation, and enjoyment is found to be significant slippage in our life in Christ. We have to be recuperated and refreshed but there are right and wholesome ways of this occurring. It can't be done by breaking the Ten Commandments, just to test their validity! Vacations are not vacations from God. We can't stop running the race and then take up where we left off two or three weeks earlier. When we do our observations of others and ourselves, don't we usually find the erosion is little by little? The monster who desires our soul is generally a timid little shrewd fellow.

The Judas Iscariots of this world are among us. We identify them not to pronounce judgment but to solidify our defense. A division into sheep and goats is the Lord's business, not ours. Thank goodness for that spiritual detail because it shows us there is a kind of holy objectivity that translates into perfect justice. The Father in his providence has made room for all of us to be judged on his terms, so that his will is always ultimately done. My suspicion is that only a few of us have known a Judas who would knowingly and deliberately betray the Christ. As we survey the field of those who may very well have disowned our Lord in open and clandestine ways, we are firmly reminded of even our possible disqualification. We are to be forgiven as we forgive others.

For some in today's world — even professing Christians — it is so hard to make them consider something with a strong negative aspect. The standard attitude is that if you are going to open your mouth, say something that makes me feel good! We hear and see so much negativism in the workaday world; we don't want to hear it in the church. All well and good, except the gospel demands that the truth be told and all Saint Paul is doing is telling the truth. Our allegiance to Christ and the church cries out for the teachings of our faith to be disseminated, as nearly as humanly possible, in all fairness. We can never provide perfect interpretations but we are not supposed to. Yet, the spirit of the law is available and it does not take a brilliant theologian to lay before us all of the help desired. The Father's mercy abounds!

Summary And Conclusion

It is imperative there is authenticity in our self-control. We can celebrate our freedom with Paul but can we also lift up the need for discipline in our lives? Time is not on our side, in fact, it is on no one's side! Again and again we discover from others and ourselves we are to be formed in the image of Christ. Our goodness and hope of heaven are directly related to the matter placed before us: We are to be a disciplined people. Furthermore, we are running a race like no other and one that has eternal consequences beyond anything else. To be possibly disqualified should make us pause in deep thought, penetrating both heart and mind.

Our life/death task is before us! Physical prowess may have little — if anything — to do with it. Superior mental capacity, while potentially providing greater dedication and service, may be a detriment. To recite all the books of the Bible and quote theology endlessly may only be an exercise in damaging pride. The big and little, handsome and not so handsome, wealthy and poor, are to be self-controlled with the living Christ in charge of our lives. Are you and I up to this demanding assignment? An old preacher once told me that for the sake of our immortal souls we had better be!

But we are not supposed to cry out how hard the road is. We are to give thanks for the opportunity. Remember, millions still have never heard about our Savior and Lord. So, the rewards of our sometimes arduous journey or race are beyond any of our imaginations.

Gift Of Positive Thinking

Introduction

For generations the "power of positive thinking" has been touted throughout our land. It is among the most popular and utilized thoughts and themes we have ever known. Cutting across all strata of social and economic patterns it is generally a principle espoused.

While the influence generated is obvious, secular and less than desirable ways of life have utilized it. It is frequently taken from a Christian basis and becomes a means to achieve ends that at a minimum are questionable. Of course, there are those who would find this line of thought simply narrow.

Saint Paul wants you and me to know and be convinced there is an idea and person far more profound than the common understanding of the "power of positive thinking." There is this gift of our Savior that makes our lives "Yes" under his lordship, always. Ultimately, there are no negatives.

Our conversion and faithful living provide a blessed safety in a sanctuary most people will not likely see. For regardless of what happens to us, the answer remains, "Yes," to all of God's promises. It is a gift far surpassing anything worldly philosophers can provide. It is always a cause and call for personal celebration with a humble spirit.

Focus

Jesus Christ alone conquers negatives.

Body

1. There is remarkable — even miraculous — power in our saying, "Yes," to Jesus.

Isn't it intriguing how some people seem to miss a victorious life in Christ by an eyelash? They never quite say the "Amen" necessary to close the deal! Yes, we have our part to play and our own free will comes in to play. With the gift being offered we are put to a test. Will we accept it or not? Our blessed Lord's arms are outstretched and some way is found to elude them. Is it a matter of a dear one deluding himself/herself? Spiritually, all pieces were in place and every butterfly was flying in formation. Failure.

My experience teaches me to begin every day with affirmations and positives that come primarily from Holy Scripture. This none-too-pleasant business of repenting of our sins of commission and omission are a required ingredient. It is a moment of setting the tone for the Lord's gift to become fully operative. What can be perceived as negatives in reality become positives. Why? Because of an exceptional power of the one who loves us far beyond our own comprehension. Even in pain of the previous day(s) we sense God is still in control and will see us through all circumstances. Again, we must accept the gift and understand it is not a tool or instrument for us to seek self-aggrandizement. If we yield to that temptation, our ministries become plighted with poisonous debris.

The gift of Christ, indeed, conquers negatives, especially as we are totally co-operative. An abundant life is there for the taking. It all sounds so easy. The best way to overcome such an easy attitude, regardless of our good spirit, is to visualize in graphic form the price that was paid for it. Only through the heinous method of crucifixion was the present of all presents granted. He was and is the propitiation for the sins of humanity, specifically you and me. What an unbelievable affront to the Savior not to accept it! The promises of the eons come together in God the Father's Son. Really, we are to do more than give thanks. We are to fall on our knees and admit none of what was and is bestowed upon us was deserved. So humility precedes thanksgiving!

It takes plenty of spiritual power in today's world to survive. Perhaps it always has. At the same time think about how in our times things can change not only quickly but radically. Who cares about yesterday's headlines? Who cares about yesterday's newspapers and magazines? There is a fluidity in persons, places, and things that stretch the imagination and often make predictions mostly nonsensical. This is why, more than ever, we must find a permanent "Yes" and cling to it at all costs. Otherwise, we keep bouncing around in ways that do not add to the quality of our spiritual lives and frequently seriously disrupt the good that is there. It may be these are spiritually the best of times and the worst of times. Our Lord wants to make the negatives positive and it can happen, praise God!

2. Life is filled with opportunities to enhance yourself and others.

Of course, this must be understood and practiced in the living stream of abundant living Saint Paul proclaims. Self-enhancement programs that must surely exist in the hundreds may lack any significant attachment to the cause of the Christian religion or the Judeo-Christian ethical system. The harm they may do is found in the reality of their goal, which is solely to produce that kind of a person who can cope in a secularized environment. As long as we live we are coping but how we do this is crucial. The apostle's message is fundamentally for those already in the fold. Yet, we must not deny its appeal to the unconverted.

In a way, there is a chasm between using and utilizing. The first is often understood as a means to get what you want, regardless of the methods employed. The second is ministering in the context of God's love and aiming for a win-win outcome. "To utilize" is to bring others into potential successes. It is to affirm one's personhood under the banner of Christ, always saying, "Yes," to him and his ways. People who feel used are seldom those who will contribute significantly to the greater good. In a sense, who can blame them, even if it happens under the auspices of the Christian faith? Much care must be taken for the sake of Christ and his church to practice the ministry of "Yes," as so graciously given to us by Paul. Anything less will cause unneeded negative sparks to fly!

Our opportunities are intended for the upbuilding of our Savior and Lord. In doing so we grow in the faith and take others with us. That is not to imply the path is free and easy or even uncomplicated. It is to maintain, and rightfully so, that Christ — in time with our obedience — conquers negatives. What a truly beautiful picture this is! The angels in heaven must be overjoyed every time they witness this happening on planet earth. Yes, and who may participate? Of course, all of Christ's sons and daughters are full partners. There are happy days (and nights) in this approach to Christian living. But be reminded, the tempter roams around, sometimes roaring like a lion, seeking to subvert our best ideas.

Is there anything in your life that is never in some way an opportunity? Perhaps, as one dear lady said, always try to make lemonade out of lemons. The worst situations that appear so bleak can become made over by the God of all of us. Since the inception of the ancient church we have seen this happen over and over. Death and destruction were present. Perhaps both occurred but who became the victor? This precious earliest of churches received the body and blood of their Lord. Then, they prepared to give their bodies and blood for the cause of Christ. Frequently, they gave their all and proved to the world the "Yes" was still valid and the faith would never be destroyed, not even temporarily. How blessed we are to have such an unrivaled heritage. Yes, all of life is one colossal opportunity and we are called to be tremendously grateful.

3. Pray that every day will be successful in God's sight.

The closing prepositional phrase in this point makes all the difference in the world, doesn't it? We are taken out of the need to have our will done. We move decisively away from setting an agenda that appeals to us. We are put in a frame of mind that opens the door to understand what God wants. In short, we remove ourselves from the center of things and events. We no longer see ourselves as the arbiter of good and bad, or right and wrong. When we pray this way in sincerity and humility, the best of all situations is born in this world. In the Pauline sense both "Yes" and "Amen" are moved to the forefront!

So why don't we pray along these lines more often? There may be as many reasons as there are personalities. Yet, there is one that tends to strike a loud chord and stick out most noticeably. We are uncomfortable — even afraid — to let loose of our will and let God be God. It is a circumstance that is not unusual. Perhaps it is best illustrated by the little boy who prays (with his hands behind his back and fingers crossed) for the good of his playmate! We know the problem, clergy and laity are summoned to keep working at it until we do better — much better. The coming of the kingdom in many lives is thwarted by those who, knowingly or unknowingly, have their crossed fingers behind their backs. "Thy kingdom come, thy will be done" awaits our humble co-operation.

We can never see things the way God does and, yet, let us not be too hasty. We do have an inkling, don't we? Sometimes we have a lot more than that, and we are surprised — even shocked — to learn what he blatantly points out to us. We admit he does not measure success the way we do. But let's don't be too hard on ourselves. When we say "Yes" to life and death, a newness in the way we perceive things and people comes about. Every day is potentially successful in God's sight. It may or may not have to do with the stock market. It may or may not have to do with promotion in one's chosen field of endeavor. It may or may not have to do with your fiancé saying the wedding is off. It may or may not have to do with your child making better grades. Just trust the Lord of all!

The gift of positive thinking is so wide-ranging it is a distinguished part of our salvation. Through our dear Lord's crucifixion and resurrection we are given the possibility of every 24 hours being successful, that is, in God's sight. As we shove our groans and grumbles aside, the glory of this stupendous way glistens like the stars in heaven. As we learn to think in certain ways, the cornucopia intended for the Father's children is at hand. Do I hear there is a celebration in order? If there isn't, there should be. Our God's vision is total and complete. Prayers born and implemented with providential perfection in our spiritual makeup enables us to participate in the greatest of all adventures: the *will* of God. What more could we possibly ask?

4. Success and failure are in the eyes of the human beholder.

As we go through life, we learn the dividing line between success and failure can become thin to the place of non-existence. It is a memorable discovery in that we dare not forget the pearl we have found! From a spiritual viewpoint this can be a major turning point in the way we view events and, in particular, people. It finally dawns on us that God decides what is success or failure. While it is humbling, there is a solid positive for all who claim Christ as Savior and Lord. For one thing, we don't have to succeed or fail on our terms. Our vision and information are so limited. For another thing we sense a profound security. It is cause for joy.

It is not easy to accept the idea that Christ conquers negatives and in doing so can make of our perceived failures an experience in success. Our Lord reminds us again and again his kingdom is not of this world; that has to do precisely with our topic at hand. At the same moment his wisdom is such that our perception of success may very well be failure which must receive the healing touch of the Master's hand. So, we hopefully cross into an arena that facilitates our every action and reaction into a great big beautiful "Yes!" Serious spirituality, I believe, is given birth by such illumination. Then, the gift of positive thinking glows in magnificence even on our bad days. Indeed, how shall anyone escape who neglects so great a salvation? Our only really conclusive failure is the rejection of Christ and the Holy Spirit on a permanent basis.

We acknowledge goals must be set and evaluations done in this world. The sometimes harsh actuality of these processes may very well send us into tantrums or to hospital beds or spur us to greater energy and focus. On the other hand, it may produce a genuine sense of success or perhaps lift us into glorious clouds of euphoria. In any event, God still loves us and will have compassion, provided we are receptive. Most of us have found ourselves in such a quandary. We have felt like asking where the presence of God is. Hopefully, it is here our cherished gift of positive thinking comes into play. Hopefully, it is also a time that we plead to God for patience, allowing neither worldly success nor failure to take the place of the here and now and eternal "Yes."

There is no substitute for the eyes of faith. Truly, it is how we see things and people that make the decisive difference in the way we live. There are different types of blindness. The spiritual kind is the worst and eventually the most influential in determining both how we live and die. Encouragement among our brothers and sisters may be the best contribution we can make to, and for, them. Please, let me help you see and, at least, partially understand God has not forsaken you. Please allow me to suggest what God may have for you. Whatever it is, he always seeks your betterment. A suggestion: refrain from saying, "I know exactly how you feel and here is God's will for you!" Our need to help and please people we love may tend to drive us in that direction.

Summary And Conclusion

To realize and fully accept our gift is a major turning point in every life that trusts in Christ's salvation. For some it may be "the" major one. More than sheer happiness is a result. One's life and death become wonderfully significant. We know beyond a doubt we have entered into that most blessed of relationships. We become established, knowing whatever happens to us, shall be well with our souls. A fulfillment, foreign to the world, is present. Our attunement with the Holy Spirit assures us we are going to touch others in a meaningful way for Christ and his church. Hurtful and unnecessary negatives are drowned in the deepest waters of the oceans. Every day will be okay because God says so!

It seems many — if not most — followers of Christ ease up to this profound truth, only to step back a pace or two. Then, in time, we bump into it again, debating whether or not to accept the gift. Such ongoing opportunity and refusal to enter into this blessed bond may well be the story of one's spiritual existence on this earth! This is not a shout for human judgment. It is a clarion call for those of us, who have accepted the gift and live by it, continually to provide ways for others to come aboard. The more we know spiritually, the more responsible we become. Away with negatives that soil our lives and those of other precious human beings! Many have been in the batter's circle too long and need to step up to the plate. To strike out or hit a home run probably does not matter. The crucial thing is we are at bat.

Making Disciples

Introduction

The fruit or lack of it in our ministries is ever before us. The truth is seen among both clergy and laity. Over a period of time it is there for others to observe and most likely evaluate. Actually, generations and centuries speak to what we have done or not done for Christ and his body, the church — visible and invisible.

Paul is inspirationally confident in the product he has labored to bring about. His work evidences a writing on their hearts, not written in ink but with the Spirit of the Living God. The proof is there. All anyone needs to do is look carefully. Those he has influenced are wonderfully valuable *letters* to the world.

It should be obvious that those professing Christ as Savior and Lord are desirous in making disciples for him. Sadly, it is not always that obvious! For reasons, known only by God for the most part, we too often provide a surface approach in our evangelistic efforts. Our lack of fruit produces a dampening expression.

Praise God, there is nothing quite like others showing the world Christ has come in their lives and we are, at least, somewhat responsible! Our concern over making our mark for the furtherance of the gospel slips into oblivion. The smallest and most colorless fruit that is genuine, changes a dreary day into something beautiful.

Focus

It is imperative to understand the proof is in the pudding.

Body

1. False advertising is an ever-present malady.

As some have maintained, anything or anyone can be made to look very good or very bad, depending upon the skill of a given promoter. I have a strong suspicion we view this happening everyday in some form or another. Of course, there is nothing new about such phenomenon, as Saint Paul recognizes. We wished it weren't true in our churches but frankly, it is seen with regularity. Sometimes repentance is needed. Some of our brothers and sisters just simply were not honest. Perhaps the purpose was to protect someone and then we learn a bit late the Lord desires the truth in love. How would the creatures in our culture go on without clever exaggeration?

It is here that clergy are summoned to take a closer look. Our own résumés may contain misleading — if not outright — misrepresentation and they are circulating! We confront a common and sometimes agonizing dilemma: Are we really that good or have we yielded to the temptation of dishonest presentation? Our competence is from God and requires thanksgiving for who and what we are, as best we can truthfully assess that. To advertise ourselves in ways we suspect or know Christ condemns is simply stupidity or close to it. Why should we even want a church or position that pragmatically calls for a problematic view of who and what we are? Of course, if we don't know who and what we are, that is a bigger problem!

At times we just promise more than we can deliver. Deep down we really and justifiably want something beneficial to come into being. What do we do? We go off the deep end and make promises out of line with the Holy Spirit. We have not actually consulted with him and therefore, have evaded the essential provision of harmony. We like to think we are doing the will of God but we are in a hurry to prove something to someone and that person is not God! We have all been there and have learned we can reap rotting fruit or even a whirlwind. Call or label it what we want, we have entered the odious field of false advertising. In a turnabout, we might not want to see the proof in the pudding!

124

Some of us have watched and experienced this desperation for nearly a half century. Forms come and go. Media expands in quality and quantity. We genuinely want good things to happen but we forget about imperative consultation with the Spirit of the Living God. Sophistication has tended to put space between those we want to help and ourselves. Clergy and laity do not need to face those for whom their message is directed, at least, not nearly to the extent we once did. In bygone days we were frequently kept honest by our close pastoral relationships. This was true in some of the largest churches. For a generation or longer there has been a tendency to remove pastors from the so-called firing line. Conditions have changed enough that accountability is most certainly a big problem. The spirit of the law is so widened and deepened we can hardly be recognized from some secular institutions!

2. The Holy Spirit has a will and ways that hopefully permeate our beings.

The history of the church shows we have gone through periods where the Holy Spirit is mostly defined as something ethereal. When the manifestation did occur, a miracle or outstanding sign of some kind seemed to be the result. Praise God, we have passed through some truly powerful times of experiencing him daily in the lives of people. It is my prayer and that of others we continue to do so! The awesomeness and beauty of the Holy Spirit in our day and time is almost more than we can handle. It is like another Day of Pentecost has come upon us. We have witnessed some glorious proof in the pudding!

Saint Paul and his co-workers knew first hand that the Spirit gives life. Disciples are made as this wonder of wonders works in the daily lives of precious people. It is indispensable in our ministries to convert others that we be permeated or at least profoundly influenced by this Spirit. As we get more and more acquainted with this force, we are sold on the authenticity that emerges for all of us to witness. We can be surprised or astounded. We can shed tears of joy or laugh out loud. This sometimes hidden and sometimes open manifestation is so moving because we know disciples are being created or being improved in their walk with the Lord.

Paul absolutely knew what he was talking about! The delightful dove moves about, providing demonstrations of day breaks.

How can we be sure we are saturated by the Spirit of the Living God? That's a tough question, isn't it? Some who claim to be led seem all too often fumbling and stumbling with little to show in a factual sense. Efforts are made, perhaps with sacrifice, and all appears to be in near perfect order. Then something or someone moves out of kilter, at least, in our assessment and our balloon bursts with an embarrassing bang. We become encouraged, only after we discover, the moment is simply a means to where the Spirit desires to take us. Our faith is tried and then days, perhaps weeks or months later, we rather sheepishly admit our myopia! There is a holy fascination about this that should greet and grip us as we give thanks.

Understanding moving at different levels aids us, doesn't it? To be honest, many of us never quite know the level we are experiencing. Yet, think how often thoroughly committed Christians come out at the same place. We are not quite sure how we got there but we got there! Our wisdom is shown for what it usually is: limited and restricted. As we accept the reality of all this, why don't we just succumb into a blessed period of positive inertia that allows for the Holy Spirit to have free reign? Really, there are moments when our best actions are no actions! We are to relax in the arms of the all-knowing and ever faithful Father of our Savior and Lord, Jesus Christ. Yes, disciples can be made this way. The Spirit will not be confined by our insistence on controlling events and assuming we are the only ones knowing God's will.

3. Discipleship is verified eventually only in flesh and blood.

So, how do we go about measuring this? That can be a problem — perhaps insurmountable — to those unsympathetic with our religion or crusty personalities who insist little or no change is probable, even in the realm of salvation. Again the eyes of faith are what make the difference. Those of us who have seen this inspirational event occur again and again do not need selling or even coaching. We have witnessed tablets of stone become tablets written on human hearts. In this case, experience is the best teacher. When we relate to a new being in flesh and blood, there can be no denial!

We all know of stories about people steeped in doctrine, who have memorized the creeds and much scripture. Unfortunately, there are examples of their hearts below the surface never being anything but stone! It suggests their practice of our precious religion is only done with their heads. It is all a matter of the brain. Our blessed Lord surely would view such a state of affairs as unhealthy and even deadly. Rules, regulations, and memorizations are means and not ends. Salvation means flesh and blood. Our Savior was not in combat with a debating society. He was showing a needy humanity he would especially give his heart for all of us. Had Jesus given us only a set of rules to follow, we would have only another philosophical system. We have infinitely more than that and an open door to heaven.

My respect for the scientific realm is considerable. In fact, let's admit science and religion are no longer mortal enemies trying to destroy one another. They haven't been for quite some time. A case in point is the part prayer plays in diseases, accidents, and the like. Studies show where prayer is seriously practiced the improvement rate is definitely higher. Throughout the health care industry there are examples galore where the two have worked together to the benefit of patients. Wholeness and holiness are frequently accepted in a context showing science and religion are partners. The strides we have made here, especially in the last two generations, have been remarkable. After all, God is the God of both!

The warmth and contentment of the Father's boys and girls — regardless of their ages — has no real substitute. We can at times see salvation in the faces of others. Our spirit bears witness to their spirit. There is a sense of both peace and vibrancy that involves heart and mind — in particular, the heart. Some would label this subjectivity and even worse. Yet, we know in the Christian religion this is paramount and gives us the proof we seek. Can we be fooled occasionally? Of course, we can. Is this reason to shy away from the Spirit that gives life and offers sermons that mostly walk and seldom talk? Yes, unquestionably yes, persons who change internally and live differently outwardly can be spotted. They can also be known and deeply appreciated by those who celebrate the oneness found in the visible and invisible church.

4. Ideally, we are an open book for others.

A bishop in the United Methodist church told his clergy that his life was an open book. Having made his trip from the militant church to the triumph church some years ago, does not lessen his testimonial. How high he would rate among our bishops would be difficult — if not impossible — to determine. Yes, and whose criteria would we use? His openness for a few of us remains intact. There was every reason to believe he was exactly that: an open book. That didn't mean he shared all the confidential material about pastors! It did mean, as a man and bishop, his life was there for all to explore. His words are like a sturdy lighthouse that refuses to go down in stormy weather.

The vulnerability of the apostle is well known. Many Jews hated him and some Christians didn't trust him. To one group he was a turncoat and to the other someone who didn't fit well at all. Nevertheless, as he persistently laid his life on the line, he must have hid nothing. He belonged first and foremost to Christ and his business was to make disciples for his Master. It was a ministry that wrote on their hearts, "Jesus Christ is Savior and Lord." He and his colleagues were ministers of a new covenant, unique and powerful for living a victorious existence here and now and forever and ever. Apparently, he liked to show and tell. You want to meet a Christian? Come and I will introduce you to one! Should we imitate him? Definitely. Can we imitate him? Yes, but be prepared to die to yourself.

For many it is increasingly problematic to sustain one's life as an open book. What we have to remember is we are dealing in spiritual matters. By its very nature, the secular world works against being fully open to anything or anyone. The disreputable are legion and trust without conditions is virtually nonexistent. Now, we are brought to terms with an essential for living as we ought to be in our day and time. In short, as nearly as possible, our vulnerable lives must be kept among those in the household of faith. That may sound like retreating from a world that desperately needs us. I don't believe it is. Even passages in our Lord's teaching convey to us we must be careful in our dealings with those who do not share our commitment.

We are not competent of ourselves and survive only by the grace of God. However, our free access is tempered by a spiritual shrewdness we had best learn to practice. As some sidewalk evangelist reminds: have a loving and open spirit but don't be stupid! We may resemble Saint Paul but we are not him and his colleagues. We do not live in the same culture. Disciples are made by common sense as well as martyr — like methodology. Being wise as serpents comes from our favorite rabbi! Yes, the proof is in the pudding but we have to be around to sample the pudding. Ideals push us forward and upward in our spiritual questing. That is good, right, proper, and beneficial. We must never lose sight of them. Ask the Lord to keep you as open as he wants you to be.

Summary And Conclusion

It is exciting to know you and I are colleagues in the making of disciples! We are all in the same boat, so to speak, in that our strength and competence are decidedly limited. But make disciples we must. Noting that our product is always found in flesh and blood should be a regular reminder. To be internally encased in steel and externally mouthing the greatness of the gospel is not acceptable. In the long run, we cannot gain others for Christ by neglecting and downplaying our need for spiritual enrichment and guidance. The call to loosen the Holy Spirit among us and live lives that invite others to become like the Master is a key task and never completely goes away.

What does it take to get our spiritual batteries charged and keep them charged? Most importantly, a humble spirit saturated by the Holy Spirit is imperative. Is there some reason to wait, perhaps because of a theological difference? In the name of God, I hope that is not the case! Always keep a vision of greeting someone in heaven because you were faithful to the Spirit of the Living God. We must not fail, dear friends, and we are so privileged just to have the opportunity at all. For countless years, pagans came and went looking for the Son of God to appear. We have no waiting to do. The opportunities are at hand. We virtually have to close our eyes not to see them. We can do better — in fact — much better in union with the Spirit. We know where the proof is.

The Transfiguration Of Our Lord
(Last Sunday After Epiphany)
2 Corinthians 4:3-6

Proclaiming Jesus Christ

Introduction
It is not easy to promote someone else. Human nature rises up against it. If we believe in our self-worth and capabilities, why should we try to sell someone else? Yes, and why should we seek to gain acceptance of a religious leader, who will eventually cause us trouble. For example, Jesus for some was not only an irritant; he was an anathema as well.

As usual, Saint Paul is not much interested in whether you like or accept him as a person. His driving mission is to proclaim Jesus Christ as Lord. He and his colleagues were slaves for the sake of Jesus. Some would call him very brave and courageous. Others would see him as a man who was ignorant — even stupid.

Unbelievers are blinded by the machinations and subtleties of this world. The light of the gospel is hidden. Paul is called to a most difficult task. He must be an agent for light to shine out of darkness. In doing so, one and only one person is to stand out. His name is Jesus Christ. Probably no one envied his assignment!

There was total commitment. If death came, so be it. For him it would be approaching a welcome exit to spend eternity with the Father's Son. Are such people around and visible today? The answer to that is up to you.

Focus
Our real mission is to make known the Christ.

Body

1. We are to rise above personal egotism for Christ's sake.

Church history tells many opportunities for conversion have been lost because a religious leader refused to enable Christ to become the center of things. He/she tragically could not give up the need to be number one. It is as though they refuse to get out from under the spotlight because that would dim their role as the one solely responsible for converting others. For those who are natural-born achievers, who crave recognition, the casualty may be quite high. Nevertheless we are not intelligent enough to know why God calls some specifically to win others, who really would rather not have the job!

Actually, whether we are low-key or quite the reverse our mission is the same. Light must shine out of darkness and we are the agents to make this happen. Our salesmanship only becomes truly successful as we sell someone other than ourselves. The whole precious program is out of line for those determined to make a name for themselves apart from the Master. Some days, even those who have accepted the slave status of servanthood discover themselves to be in revolt. It is so against our natural inclinations the best disciples struggle to be at peace with their real mission. Where you and I find ourselves is crucial to our continuing in the faith and being fruitful in spreading the light to others.

The temptation is not to tell the old, old story of Jesus and his love but to tell our story in an effort to secure status. Recall our Lord's temptations in the desert. Pastors — in particular — are vulnerable. A human personality, rich in goodness, has a natural attraction. It is a little like the layperson who talks about wanting to go and hear *so and so* preach. That sounds so innocent and complimentary, until we note the preacher seems to be in first place and worshiping God in second place or lower. Christ is intended to be proclaimed, not the best and most likable preacher in a nearby city. Is that a bit of a stretch? My experience says popular preachers are to be on guard. The proclamation of our Savior and Lord is the one and only top priority.

The really big battles pastors face are almost always internal. The wars are sometimes fierce, as we labor to keep ourselves out of the limelight. The shrewdness of Satan, let's face it, outwits us and there we are with our names in bold letters, just above "Proclaiming the Christ!" It's funny and yet it isn't because so much is at stake. Pastors cannot — strictly speaking — win others to themselves, establishing a following, and expect to do the will of God. We are instruments and means. We are not the ends of much of anything because of a simple fact: we are mortal, being created and not the creator. To be sure, for those of us who have been in ministry this is common ground. Yet, how quickly we can yield to the temptation of placing ourselves first. We are called to be on guard.

2. We are to take slave status that provides a clear image of the Christ.

How can cherished human beings in the sight of God see, unless we are obedient and work to remove dangerous and even deadly cataracts? Spiritual eyesight, when it is faulty, gives birth to distortions that lead others in wrong directions. Not only do they arrive at dead ends, they take others with them. Correctives are amazing in some cases. Why? Because Christians are willing to walk the second mile in helping others see better, hopefully a spiritual 20/20! As we cooperate with the Holy Spirit, we recognize the strength given to us by the one who has all the strength there ever was, is, and shall be. Our full cooperation can give truly amazing results.

Slavery can take on a purely negative connotation. That must never happen under the lordship of our Savior and Lord! It is noteworthy some thinkers have insisted we will be a slave of someone or something. Frequently it is our self-will and righteousness. For others it may be full commitment to a political, economic, or social ideology. Some intellectuals throughout recorded history have led countless people in directions far from the salvation of God's Son. Witness the catastrophic effects of communism that often espoused atheism. Some started off in the right direction, only to depart and relegate the Christian religion to a miscellaneous place in life. Obviously, the kingdom of God they proclaimed was not at all like that of our Christ. Praise God, you and I have a blessed slavery.

In a profound sense, we are also slaves for others. Just like our Good Shepherd, we are to lay down our lives for lost sheep. Perhaps we have not seen that much at work in our lifetimes. It is far more connected with the ancient church and those martyred witnesses that have been in all ages, including the present. In the foreign mission fields there are true stories that are heartbreaking. Even an elementary understanding of human rights is cast aside. The killing and prior suffering are almost beyond comprehension. How can this happen in a world that is supposed to be civilized? Our answer is not difficult. Whenever we get totally serious about Jesus Christ in some cultures all hell breaks loose!

Saint Paul was such a strange fellow. He found full meaning to his life and death in the blessedness of Christlike slavery! His mission, painfully human as it was, never seemed to deviate from making Christ known. While there are others in the gallery of the saints who may have a more prominent place, we may want to look carefully. Some might even compare him to a good terrorist ready, willing, and able to be blown up in order to remove barriers that get in the way of receiving Christ. Perhaps that moves beyond our best sensitivities, but think about it a while. To be sure it is suicidal, but martyrdom has always been seen in some people's eyes as unneeded and a way to die bravely because the person did not want to go on living. Problematic? Yes, but it may be an avenue of opening dialogue with radical Muslims.

3. We are to lose ourselves in Christ for his cause.

When we begin to lose ourselves in anything, we tend to fight back. That's true eventually even in the jobs we love or the movement we are convinced is right, true, and just. Regardless of the great love our Savior bestows upon us, there is fear and apprehension of losing ourselves. The scriptures tell us that to lose ourselves for the purpose of finding ourselves is imperative. Still, our tendency is to revolt and I suspect — if the truth were known — that is exactly what happens in most cases. Of course, the saints in their words and actions make abundantly clear that the most completely powerful way to proclaim Christ is by being absorbed by his love that knows no bounds.

When we examine our lives with full honesty, we probably make a discovery that brings a sense of failure. We want Christ as Savior and Lord with all our hearts, minds, and souls but are unable or mostly unwilling to move beyond that. The way things are is just fine. Others note our exemplary lives and we feel fulfilled. When we are making an obvious contribution on behalf of Christ and the church, why grow anymore? Some even say that if it isn't broke, why fix it? Common sense and pride say to leave well enough alone. So, our proclamation rates above the average in our biased inspections. When I already have all of this, why should I want more? The apostle says it isn't enough, until our proclamation is fully unfettered.

Are we moving along lines that are not all that important? No. Why? Because the purpose is to proclaim Jesus Christ and that is only supremely done by losing ourselves in him. Is there room for compromise? Of course and there always is. You and I may very well choose that broad pathway like countless others. If we do, let's admit to ourselves what we have done and not claim the opportunity was never presented. Full commitment and spiritual success go hand-in-hand. Being lost in Christ is full commitment. In college we used to joke about being a "B" or "C" student and not to take the trouble of striving for an "A." Who needs the increased dedication and hard work? Employers are not looking for intellectuals who have no practical judgment, so let's play it safe. Just who are we attempting to fool?

The Christian is to be in a growth pattern all of his/her life. Our real mission of making Christ known can be perfected, until the day the death angel greets us. While we know this is true, there is invariably the temptation to avoid and evade by methods both subtle and not so subtle. The aim is never a better place in heaven. However, some of us who strive to be fully in Christ are accused of that very thing. We can even be described as holier-than-thou disciples who want to outdo others and wear a more expensive crown! They are annoyed by us and sometimes will deliberately stay away from us. This happens not only among laity but among the ordained clergy as well. Sometimes the negative politics of the clergy can be demonic, as pastors are pushed into patterns which do not proclaim Jesus Christ.

4. We are to give thanks for the part we can play.

Thanksgiving is built into Saint Paul's writings, perhaps like no other's in Holy Scripture. Is there ever a place in our lives with Christ that giving thanks is unneeded or perhaps out of order? For me that answer is a firm, "No." To live in Christ, proclaiming him with every facet of our being, means if everything has not turned out right, it ultimately will. The saints have maintained and lived by this, regardless of the situations in which they found themselves. Greatness glistens before our eyes, as Christ is proclaimed, in ways that are frequently miraculous and beyond human understanding. Sorry to say, in our often partially dedicated lives, we are thankful when most things are going right for us!

The corpus of Pauline writing shows a man so thankful that some probably inquired about his sanity. How can anyone go through what he did and continually give thanks just to be a vessel for promoting someone else? The normal attitude is to insist that if we are going to do the hard work and suffering, then we are going to get the credit. After all, isn't that the only really fair way to handle one's life? Well, it does certainly sound equitable for all concerned, that is, until we seriously come to terms with our Savior and Lord. He wants all of us — today, tomorrow, and forever! He calls us to come and die to ourselves that the Lord may be fully proclaimed through our lives. It is asking a lot and only a little because to be held in his embrace is the apex of happiness.

For the Christian, every minute of every day ought to be filled with thanksgiving. The chief reason is the promise God will never leave us or forsake us. International figures with military power and so much money they can't count it find themselves excluded from such security. There is a value system here that confounds the world and always has. Indeed, how can anyone lose himself and find himself? The only sense it makes to the world is the failure to actualize oneself into his/her own authority figure that gains the respect of secular society. If one gets lost and loses control of life, what is left but a series of failed attempts to be somebody — as defined by worldly values? No wonder we people who totally commit ourselves to Christ appear to be a bunch of idiots!

Nothing quite paves and prepares the way for accepting Christ as an unbridled attitude of gratitude. Aren't the people in your church, who really inspire and motivate you, filled with gratitude? To be one of spiritual depth and ungrateful is a contradiction. Of the thousands of parishioners I have known over many years — to my mind — there are no exceptions. Disciples of Christ are naturally and spontaneously thankful. Take another look at your church and tell me what you find. Okay, take a careful not a cursory look! All days are for thanksgiving, especially in the life of the one, holy, catholic, and apostolic church. The knowledge of the glory of God in the face of our redeemer is also our glory as our faces shine like stars in a troubled universe. Brothers and sisters we have a privileged place!

Summary And Conclusion

Every person in life has a mission, spoken or unspoken. It is doubtful some even recognize it, until their later years. Nevertheless, there it is and for a few more than one mission makes up their lives, depending on their age and conditions. As disciples of Jesus Christ we know where we stand. The questions are all answered about this matter. Day in and day out we proclaim him. It is part of the air we breathe. In joys and sorrows, failures and successes, thanksgivings prevail as we shout or whisper his name. It becomes our chief reason for being and communicates to others how we see our lives and deaths. Our driving duty is to let light shine out of darkness.

Praises be to God who comes to us as Father, Son, and Holy Spirit, doubts are settled and we are grateful for the challenge we have accepted. Friends, if you have delayed in accepting the only mission that ultimately counts, please reconsider. If need be, retrace your steps and try to discover where you refused to accept this awesome adventure. Review, as long as you need to, your life. Then come to terms with the invitation that is still being given. My experience is the dear Lord comes to us with a holy pressure, uncomfortable though it be which is always for our benefit. So, as all prophets and evangelists have persistently declared: today is the day of salvation. Indeed, today is just right — if you have not done so — to promise the Father all the rest of your days will be spent proclaiming Jesus Christ, as Savior and Lord. We Christians are so fortunate. In the long run we are never losers!

LaVergne, TN USA
13 November 2009
164011LV00002B/1/P